Herbert Railton, William J. Loftie

A Brief Account of Westminster Abbey

abridged from the larger work

Herbert Railton, William J. Loftie

A Brief Account of Westminster Abbey
abridged from the larger work

ISBN/EAN: 9783348022385

Printed in Europe, USA, Canada, Australia, Japan

Cover: Foto ©Lupo / pixelio.de

More available books at **www.hansebooks.com**

A BRIEF ACCOUNT OF

WESTMINSTER ABBEY

ABRIDGED FROM THE LARGER WORK

BY

W. J. LOFTIE, B.A., F.S.A.

Author of " WINDSOR CASTLE," " A HISTORY OF LONDON,"
&c., &c.

With Illustrations by
HERBERT RAILTON

LONDON
SEELEY AND CO. LIMITED
ESSEX STREET, STRAND
1894

RICHARD CLAY & SONS, LIMITED,
LONDON & BUNGAY.

CONTENTS

		PAGE
I.	THORNEY .	1
II.	THE MINSTER .	12
III.	THE MINSTER (*continued*)	23
IV.	CORONATIONS .	37
V.	THE CONFESSOR'S CHAPEL	48
VI.	THE CHAPEL OF HENRY VII. .	61
VII.	THE TRIFORIUM	77
VIII.	THE POETS' CORNER AND THE CHAPTER-HOUSE	90
IX.	THE HERALDRY	103
X.	THE MONUMENTS .	112
XI.	THE EPITAPHS .	126
XII.	A WALK IN THE PRECINCTS .	141

LIST OF ILLUSTRATIONS

PAGE

QUEEN ELEANOR'S TOMB. BY H. RAILTON (*Frontispiece*)

WESTMINSTER HALL AND ABBEY. AFTER HOLLAR 3

WESTMINSTER ABBEY FROM DEAN'S YARD. BY H. RAILTON . . 7

THE ENTRANCE TO POETS' CORNER. BY H. RAILTON 9

SOUTH TRANSEPT OF WESTMINSTER ABBEY. BY H. RAILTON. . 15

VIEW FROM DARK CLOISTER. BY H. RAILTON. 17

EDWARD THE CONFESSOR'S CHAPEL, NOW THE PIX OFFICE. BY
H. RAILTON 19

WESTMINSTER ABBEY FROM THE NORTH-EAST. BY H. RAILTON. 25

CLOISTER GARTH. BY H. RAILTON 29

THE DEANERY. BY H. RAILTON 33

THE INTERIOR OF THE NAVE. BY H. RAILTON . . . 39

TOMBS IN THE SACRARIUM. BY H. RAILTON 43

THE CORONATION CHAIR AND SCREEN. BY H. RAILTON 45

THE CONFESSOR'S CHAPEL. BY H. RAILTON 49

SOUTH AISLE OF THE CHOIR. BY H. RAILTON 51

TOMB OF RICHARD II. BY H. RAILTON 55

HENRY VII.'S CHAPEL (INTERIOR). BY H. RAILTON . . 63

HENRY VII.'S SHRINE. AFTER HOLLAR 65

ONE BAY OF HENRY VII.'S CHAPEL. BY H. RAILTON . . . 67

EFFIGIES OF HENRY VII. AND QUEEN 69

PAGE

FAN VAULTING IN SOUTH AISLE OF HENRY VII.'S CHAPEL. BY
    H. RAILTON 71

TOMB OF QUEEN MARY STUART 72

MONUMENT OF QUEEN ELIZABETH 73

HENRY VII.'S CHAPEL. LOOKING WEST. BY H. RAILTON . . . 75

THE CHOIR. BY H. RAILTON 81

TWO BAYS OF TRIFORIUM. BY H. RAILTON 83

CHAUCER'S TOMB. BY H. RAILTON 91

POETS' CORNER. BY H. RAILTON 95

THE CHAPTER-HOUSE. BY H. RAILTON 97

HENRY VII.'S CHAPEL (EXTERIOR). BY H. RAILTON . . . 109

THE THREE CANNINGS 115

MONUMENT OF DEAN STANLEY 123

NORTH AISLE OF THE CHOIR. BY H. RAILTON 129

THE NORTH TRANSEPT. BY H. RAILTON 143

Westminster Abbey

I

THORNEY

The Site of Westminster—The Thames Side—The Local Names—London in 886—The Thorn Ey—The Watling Street—The Tyburn—The Abbey—*Locus Terribilis*—Contrast with St. Denis—The Confessor's Abbey—Architecture—Historical Summary—A French Visitor a Hundred Years Ago.

IF we could survey the site of Westminster as it was in, say, the time of King Alfred, we might be able to solve some modern geographical problems.   It is not possible, unfortunately, to draw a complete picture of the place as it was a thousand years ago ; yet, by chance, some very ancient materials exist—materials into whose age and authenticity we may have occasion to inquire in another chapter ; but they enable us to mark distinctly some important points, around which we can build a more or less useful working hypothesis.

We may take our stand near the Thames side.   The river here is very wide and very shallow.   As the tide rolls up from the sea it floods vast muddy tracts on both sides, and the very ancient names which survive show us where were the small spots of land over which the river or the tide did

B

not usually wash. A little higher up on the other side was Batter's, perhaps Peter's, Ey. We know that an ey is an island. There are many ways of spelling it. Thus we have Winchelsea, Sheppey, and Ely, in each of which the same word is spelt differently. Close to Thorney was, and is, Chelsea, the island of chesils, or flint gravel. A little nearer was the Lamb Hithe, now Lambeth. We know that a hithe is a landing-place. There are many on the lower Thames, Garlickhithe, Rotherhithe, and so on. Immediately opposite to where we are standing is the Stane Gate. We know that stane, or stan, meant stone, and that gate, or geat, was a road. These are all very old names, and may be taken to denote firm places in the waste of low tidal marsh on the Surrey shore.

On the Middlesex shore, also, we have some very venerable names, and starting with the assumption that every name has its meaning, and gives its little contribution to the whole history of the place, we may examine them carefully.

We are standing, then, on a low sandy hillock, surrounded at high tide by water, except where a causeway joins it to a higher hillock standing nearly due west of it. As the stream sweeps past we look down its course and see it bend to the eastward about half a mile off, and a mile further, beyond the bend, is a bridge, and on both sides of the river are low walls with towers and semi-circular bastions, within which we may perhaps descry a few red roofs and a few shingled church-spires. One in particular is more conspicuous than the rest, both because it is the nearest, and also because it is the greatest. That church within the walls is the 'Minster of St. Paul, in London,' as it is often called, even as far back as a thousand years ago.

In 886, we know, King Alfred refounded London, repaired

Parliment House   the Hall   the Abby

Ciuitalis Weftmonafterieus is pars

WESTMINSTER HALL AND ABBEY. AFTER HOLLAR.

the walls and bridge, and instituted some kind of government. All the country round had been desolated by the Danes, and was probably lying fallow and as nearly in its primitive state as at any time since the Saxon conquest. The hillock on which we stand is called Thorn-Ey. There are some Roman remains on it, and there may have been the ruins of a little monastery and chapel, of which floating traditions were afterwards gathered and exaggerated. The paved causeway to the westward is the Watling Street. On both sides of it runs the Tyburn, of which Thorn-Ey is a kind of delta. The road rises to Tot Hill, which is a conspicuous landmark here, and goes straight on over the 'Bulunga Fen' till it reaches another, the 'road to Reading,' which has just crossed the Tyburn at Cowford, where Brick Street is now in Piccadilly.

We may conclude, if we wish to do so, that in a sense Westminster is older than London itself. What name it was called by we know not; but the Romans certainly had a station here, as I have said, and the importance of the place before the making of London Bridge may have been considerable. There is nothing known about it, however, and we must begin with the foundation of the institution which has made the Thorney, under its later name, so famous in out English annals.

The Abbey, with its church and the houses surrounding it, was destined to play a more prominent part in the history of King Alfred's descendants and the people whose land he rescued from the Danes, than any other in his realm. The mediaeval monks, in trying to make it out to be as old as possible, contrived so utterly to defeat their ends that we cannot now tell how old it really is. The legend of King Seberht was probably invented in the reign of

Henry III., and was not more distinctly a fiction than many others of the same period which had more serious conse- quences. If we admit the fact of the foundation of an abbey here by Seberht, or some other potentate, before the Danish invasion, we may, perhaps, take it to account for the idea prevalent long afterwards that Thorney was a *locus terribilis*, a sacred or venerable spot. Professor Middleton, one of the best authorities, suggests this inter- pretation, and refers us to the words of Jacob (Genesis xxviii. 17) where he says of Bethel, *Quam terribilis est locus iste!* King Edward the Confessor is made to refer to the same passage in a poem on his life; when speaking of Westminster he continues the quotation from Genesis: 'Non est hic aliud nisi . . . porta cœli'—'This is the gate of heaven.'

From the reign of Edward, at latest, Westminster became the head-quarters of the King's government; and the Abbey and its church, rather than the Church of St. Paul in London or the metropolitan church at Canterbury, the religious centre of the nation. From the day when Harold, still full of hopes of success against the Norman invader, here assumed the Crown, to the day when Queen Victoria came to offer solemn thanksgiving for her reign of half a century, the Church of St. Peter has been the scene of the highest ceremonials in our land. In this respect no other place can equal it in interest. It has been the St. Denis of England, and something more. At St. Denis the ungrateful mob destroyed the tombs and insulted the dead bodies of the old kings of France. Its restoration has been of the most conjectural kind; and the visitor sees little or nothing that is not perfectly new. At Westminster our kings have slept in peace; only disturbed now and then by the in-

quisitiveness of some peeping official, bent on obtaining
knowledge at the expense of reverence. Of all the styles
of architecture illustrated in Westminster Abbey, the one we
most miss is the Norman, but the Chapel of St. Katharine
adjoining the Infirmary was of that period; and in other
places we see every variety of Pointed style, from the half
French apse of Henry III. to the delicately proportioned
Gothic of Sir Christopher Wren, carried out by Hawksmoor
or James, his pupils, in the two western towers. The work
he superintended, or, at least, sanctioned, in the north
transept has lately, I regret to say, been 'restored'—that
is, destroyed; but to me, at least, it was very interesting,
as the latest attempt to carry on the Gothic tradition in
English architecture.

The visitor from Australia or America feels his English
blood more thoroughly stirred in Westminster Abbey than
anywhere else in our island. It is something which makes
history real and tangible to stand beside the actual tomb
of the distant and shadowy King and Saint whose weakness
and vanity betrayed England to the Norman. Almost on
the same spot the Conqueror was crowned after his victory
at Senlac, near Hastings. The old Norman church disappeared under Henry III. When we stand by Henry's
gorgeous tomb, with its porphyry inlay and its mosaics, we
recollect that the false and feeble heart is not here, but at
Fontevraud; yet his career affords a remarkable example
of the fact that the most exquisite taste in matters artistic
may exist in the same mind with everything that is despicable.
In days when people talk so glibly of the disintegration of
the Empire, and even of the Kingdom, it does one good
to read the 'Pactum Serva' of the great lawgiver who smote
the separatist Scots of his day. There is the stone he

Westminster Abbey from Dean's Yard.

brought from Scotland,—the stone which the men of that
time and long after firmly believed to have been the same
on which Jacob had laid his head in that other *locus terribilis*
in the Holy Land beyond the sea. What more appropriate
gift could he bring to 'the Gate of Heaven'? The old
age of Edward III. and the decay of the kingdom become
a reality to us as we gaze at his effigy with its venerable
beard. Near it, too, is the gilded tomb of his unfortunate
grandson, and we remember that in his time the Clerk of
the Works in the Abbey was Geoffrey Chaucer, that he
lived a little to the eastward, where we now see the chapel
of Henry VII., and that he is buried here—the father of
English poets—among his intellectual descendants in the
Poets' Corner. High overhead we still see the memorials
of the nation's mourning for the death of Henry V. in the
relics of his state funeral—the most imposing ceremonial of
the kind ever seen in England until that day. From tomb
to tomb, from chapel to chapel, we seem to be floating
down the stream of time, between walls which are the
petrifaction of our history, a solemn and solid witness and
testimony to the acts of great men, to the facts of great
events, and, above all, to that continuity of cause and effect
which links us with the far-away times of Edward the
Confessor and Harold the son of Godwin, and beyond them
again to the days of Alfred, the great progenitor of our
English kings, before Thorney had become Westminster.

Westminster Abbey has always been and continues to be
a 'show place.' Pepys visited it two hundred years ago and
was gulled by his guide. We can never forget the visit of Sir
Roger de Coverley, as described by Addison. A less known
visitor was the French author of an account of a trip to
England in 1788, just a century ago. It is unfortunately

The Entrance to Poet's Corner

anonymous. The writer passed twenty-one days in London, and was evidently well pleased with the place and its inhabitants. Of Westminster Abbey he has much to say. 'It was with a holy respect,' he writes, 'seized with religious emotion, that I made the tour of the *majestueuse église.*' 'There,' he continues, 'repose the ashes of heroes who have been praised to you from your infancy, whom you have followed through battles, who defended their God, their country, their children, without any pretence of seeking *la gloire.*' He found great fault with some of the monuments as badly designed, badly executed, and in bad taste, and yet he saw an Englishman take his son up to one of the worst of them, and heard him praising the hero it commemorated. Then he watched as the boy's eye brightened, his face grew animated, his cheek turned pale with excitement. All this the Frenchman notes with a blush at his adverse criticisms. He greatly praises the choir. His notes on the monuments are valuable, as showing that even a hundred years ago, before the wars of the Napoleon epoch had so greatly increased their number, they were already by far too large, ugly and vulgar. The monument of General Wolfe was new then, and the 'pan-cake monument' not old. He makes many comments on the flags, which apparently then hung in the choir. But the point on which he dwells with most satisfaction is the Poets' Corner.

In the pages on Westminster Abbey which follow the present chapter, I shall not attempt any complete history of the church. The subject would be too large for my limits, and has already been treated of many times. I can refer the reader for a history to Brayley, and for a guide to the admirable little handbook prepared by the daughters of the present Dean. But there are many things to be noticed

which do not necessarily enter into either a history or a
guide, and to them I hope to direct the reader's attention, as,
for example, to the meaning and ceremonial of coronations,
to the significance of the architecture, to the art displayed
in the royal tombs, to the early and interesting examples
of heraldry to be found on the walls, and to the history of
English epitaphs as illustrated by the monuments. These
are some of the subjects on which I hope to touch; to do
justice to such a theme as Westminster Abbey is, unfortunately, a task which would try the powers of a much more
graphic pen than mine.

II

THE MINSTER

Dimensions of Thorney—The Precincts—Legends of the Foundation—Offa
—Pious Frauds—West Minster—Edgar—The Boundaries—Edward
the Confessor—The New Foundation—The Church—The Cloister—
Remains of Edward's Buildings—The Dark Cloister—The Chapel of
the Pyx—The Church Consecrated—The Legend of Seberht.

THORNEY may be defined as an island lying off the
coast of Middlesex in the estuary of the Thames. It
was very scientifically described for us about half a century
ago by William Bardwell, of Park Street, Westminster, one
of the architects of the 'Westminster Improvement Company.'
He says it is about 470 yards long and 370 yards wide, and
is washed on the east side by the Thames, on the south by
a rivulet running down College Street, on the north by another
stream, which flows, or flowed, through Gardener's Lane, the
two being joined by the 'Long Ditch,' which formed a western
boundary, as nearly as possible where Prince's Street is now.
Within the narrow limits thus described stand both the Abbey
and the Houses of Parliament and various other familiar
public buildings which need not be enumerated here. The
precincts were formerly surrounded by stone walls, of which
a fragment may still be seen here and there, and were entered

by four noble gateways, three of which have perished. One of them was at King Street, and was combined with a bridge over the brook at Gardener's Lane. Another, also with a bridge, was at College Street. The bridge is far below the present pavement. The third, opening on Tothill Street, was still in part standing fifty years ago, but the Gate-house prison adjoining was demolished in 1777. The fourth gate was in a wall which divided the Palace from the Abbey at New Palace Yard. A modern representative of the College Street gate still exists.

The 'Venerable Beda,' who died in 736, or thereabouts, does not mention Westminster in his 'Ecclesiastical History,' and Widmore is probably right when he lays down the facts of the case, and dates the Abbey between 730 and 740, adding that, in his opinion, there is no authority for the story that Seberht founded it, and that the first authors known to have 'delivered this account' lived at least 450 years after the time assigned, and, moreover, do not agree among themselves. He sums up the whole question thus :—'There were strong reasons, both from interest and the practice of these times, when, I suppose, the story was first made, to induce the monks of Westminster not to be content with such an early foundation for their monastery as it actually had, but to assign to it the very earliest they could think of, and to make and invent histories for this purpose, as their successors did some time afterwards forge charters on a like occasion, to support a claim to privilege and an exemption from episcopal supervision.'

The practice here alluded to by Widmore was undoubtedly very common in the Middle Ages. The pious fraud was not easily detected in those days. The monks kept the seal of

the Confessor, the first English king, it is believed, who used
a seal, and could affix it to any document. The proud Abbey
of Westminster, under its immediate royal patrons, was always
galled at the idea that the other 'minster,' St. Paul's, was ever
so much older, and, indeed, dated from the period of the first
introduction of Christianity. A student of local names would,
however, apart from all historical or documentary evidence,
ask the meaning of the words 'West Minster,' and whether
they do not point to the previous existence of another
'minster' to the eastward. The word 'minster,' or, in Latin,
'monasterium,' is constantly applied to both St. Paul's and
St. Peter's; and if the charter of Offa may be relied upon,
in his day the building on Thorney had already been
distinguished from the older building within London wall as
Westminster.

As to the reason why this is not the parish of St. Peter, but
of St. Margaret, I shall have something to say in a subsequent
chapter. It is referred to in Domesday as 'the land of St.
Peter of Westminster,' and we are told that the Abbot had in it
thirteen hides and a half. There was arable land enough for
eleven ploughs, pasture for the cattle of the town, and wood
for a hundred pigs. Besides this rural estate the Abbot had
twenty-five houses for 'his knights and other men.' The word
in the original for 'knights' is 'milites,' and may denote
soldiers or servants—'knechts.'

The great difficulty in finding a date for the Abbey is further
complicated by the events which occurred during the Danish
invasion. The marauders who shut up the King within the
walls of London and ravaged the whole land, and who murdered
the Archbishop at Greenwich, are not likely to have spared the
little Abbey on Thorney. It is tolerably certain, though not

South Transept

actually proved, that Dunstan, by bringing twelve Benedictine monks from Glastonbury and planting them at Westminster, practically founded the Abbey, which, however, does not appear to have been in a very flourishing condition down to the time of Edward the Confessor ; and there seems at one period, where there is a blank in the list of Abbots, to have been no community here at all. This may well have been the case, as I have said, during the Danish invasion of 1012. We find it receiving the Manor of Hampstead from King Ethelred in 986, and other lands from a certain Leofwine in 998 ; so that if the monks fled during the troubles, they must have come back again, because they were in possession of these estates at a later period. The Danish King Harold was buried in their church in 1042, but his body was subsequently dug up and flung into the Thames by his unnatural brother Hardicnut. To Hardicnut succeeded his half-brother Edward, and prosperity began to smile on Westminster Abbey.

The new King took up his abode close by, and built himself a splendid palace, of which the contemporary remains in Westminster Hall are a sufficient witness. Dean Stanley well names Edward as 'the last of the Saxons and the first of the Normans,' and his buildings here were probably the first examples of the Norman style that had been seen. It was in fulfilment of a vow that he rebuilt the Abbey. He had intended to make a pilgrimage to the grave of St. Peter at Rome, but was absolved by the Pope on condition he should found or restore a monastery of St. Peter. Westminster stood ready to hand. Its Abbot, Eadwine, was a favourite courtier, and the buildings were pressed forward with speed, and were, we are told, completed in about fifteen years.

Of the Confessor's Abbey a few fragments are still extant.

The church was in the form of a cross—a novelty in design
in England—and had many pillars and arches. What such a
church was like we may gather from the Bayeux tapestry,

View from
Dark Cloisters

where it is represented at large. The nave, which was not,
however, finished so soon, consisted of five bays, arched, and
at the crossing of the transepts there was a taller arch of the

c

same width. The east end, as in the not much later chapel
in the White Tower, was semi-circular. The old church was
left standing, not to interrupt the services, and must have
been somewhere to the westward. Only the choir was finished
at the time of Edward's death, and the end of the nave, with
its towers, was not built. It must have been quite as wide as
the present church—'an opinion,' says Sir Gilbert Scott, in the
'Gleanings,' 'which is, to a certain extent, corroborated by the
size of the Cloister Court, the north and east sides of which
would have been defined by the external walls of the nave and
the dormitory, and its south limits by the refectory, in which
there exist early remnants sufficient to show that it occupies
the original site.' If we complete the square thus indicated
we have evidence that the nave was within three bays of the
length of the present nave, and it was probably quite as long.

It is on account of the preservation of the Confessor's plan
that the western aisle of the south transept is wanting, its space
being occupied by the cloister. The chamber immediately
above is used as a muniment-room for the archives of the
church, and contains some very ancient chests, decorated with
iron-work, some of which date from the thirteenth century.

The monastery, as distinguished from the church, lay on the
south side, and here remains of the Confessor's work may
readily be recognised. The so-called 'Dark Cloister' is the
best known. It is the substructure of the Dormitory, a square
hole in the vaulting 'restored' away a few years ago, admitting
a rude stair. When Edward raised the number of monks to
seventy he had, of course, to provide sufficient accommodation,
and this part of his building is peculiarly massive, but devoid of
ornament. 'Several of its walled-up windows are visible in the
great school.' One exterior window remains little altered.

Below this building is the 'Chapel of the Pyx,' an apartment seldom or never seen by a visitor. Sir Gilbert Scott speaks of the difficulty he experienced in obtaining admission. It was,

Edward the Confessors Chapel now Pyx Office.

he says, 'a formidable visit, requiring the presence of representatives of the Treasury and the Exchequer, with their attendants bearing boxes which contain six mighty keys.' This used to be a treasury, and still contains the empty coffers, the Pyx alone being stored in it now. What is the Pyx? The word is etymologically the same as 'box,' means a chest or case in which something precious is deposited. Here it is the coin of the realm of which specimens are kept, and the new coin annually tried by them before a jury of experts.

The Confessor's work, so far as it was finished, was consecrated just before his death. Mr. Freeman well says, 'the royal saint deemed himself set upon the throne, not to secure the welfare or the independence of his kingdom, but to build a church and endow a monastery in honour of the Prince of the Apostles.' The King was too ill to take any part in the ceremony to which he had looked forward all his reign. Before the Christmas Festival was over the new church 'beheld the funeral rites of its founder, and the coronation rites of his successor.'

I have thus endeavoured to sketch the early history of Westminster Abbey. It is impossible not to agree with a remark of Dart's on this subject. He says:—'There is, I think, no church whose original has afforded more various matters of conjecture than this; and those who have earnestly contended for her antiquity have so clouded that time with fables that we scarce know where to find it.'

Let us turn back for an instant and see what was the universally received legend of the Middle Ages about it.

There was in the Roman time on Thorney a temple of Apollo. Then came the Christian king, Lucius, and founded the Church of St. Peter upon Cornhill, and the Abbey of St. Peter upon Thorney. But in process of time the Christian Britons were conquered and driven away by the heathen Saxons, and St. Peter's upon Thorney was destroyed. At length a king named

Seberht arose, and reigned over the East and Middle Saxons.
He founded the Church of St. Paul in London. This is a
fact attested by the almost contemporary Beda. But, said the
monks of Westminster, he also founded their Abbey, and was
buried in their church. Dean Stanley thus narrates the
legend :—

'It was on a certain Sunday night, in the reign of King Sebert, the eve of
the day fixed by Mellitus, first Bishop of London, for the consecration of
the original monastery in the Isle of Thorns, that a fisherman of the name
of Edric was casting his nets from the shore of the island into the Thames.
On the other side of the river, where Lambeth now stands, a bright light
attracted his notice. He crossed, and found there a venerable personage,
in foreign attire, calling for some one to ferry him over the dark stream.
Edric consented. The stranger landed, and proceeded at once to the church,
standing ready for its impending consecration. The air suddenly became
bright with a celestial splendour. The building stood out clear, "without
darkness or shadow." A host of angels, descending and re-ascending, with
sweet odours and flaming candles, assisted, and the church was dedicated
with the usual solemnities. The fisherman remained in his boat, so awe-
struck by the sight that when the mysterious visitant returned and asked
for food he was obliged to reply that he had caught not a single fish. Then
the stranger revealed his name :—"I am Peter, keeper of the keys of
heaven. When Mellitus arrives to-morrow, tell him what you have seen ;
and show him the token that I, St. Peter, have consecrated my own Church
of St. Peter, Westminster, and have anticipated the Bishop of London.
For yourself, go out into the river : you will catch a plentiful supply of
fish, whereof the larger part shall be salmon. This I have granted on two
conditions—first, that you never fish again on Sundays ; secondly, that you
pay a tithe of them to the Abbey of Westminster."
'The next day, at dawn, the Bishop Mellitus rises, and begins to prepare
the anointing oils and the utensils for the great dedication. He, with the
King, arrives at the appointed hour. At the door they are met by Edric,
with the salmon in his hand, which he presents from St. Peter in a gentle
manner to the Bishop. He then proceeds to point out the marks of the
twelve crosses on the church, the walls within and without moistened with
holy water, the letters of the Greek alphabet written twice over distinctly on
the sand of the now sacred island, "the traces of the oil and (chiefest of
the miracles) the droppings of the angelic candles." The Bishop professed

himself entirely convinced, and returned from the church "satisfied that the dedication had been performed sufficiently, better, and in a more saintly fashion than a hundred such as he could have done."'

This charming legend needs no refutation. It is interesting, both as a pretty story and also as showing what, in spite of the marvellous civilisation of the thirteenth century, in which it was composed, people could be got to believe in those days.

III

THE MINSTER (*continued*)

The Canonisation of Edward—The Parish of St. Margaret—The Abbey
Estates—Kensington Palace—Henry III.—How the Confessor was
Commemorated—The New Church—Its Consecration—Tothill Fair—
The Chantry of Henry V.—The Nave—Two Removals—A Great
Robbery—The Last Abbot—Dean Goodman.

THE church built by Edward was destined to stand for
almost exactly two centuries. It was consecrated in
1065, and its successor in 1269. Midway between these two
dates, in 1163, the Confessor was canonised, ninety-two years
after his death. Even before that time his grave was venerated.
Dean Bradley has well summarised the reasons which united
by chance to make one of the least estimable of English kings
to be literally worshipped within a hundred years of his death.
The passage occurs on page 2 of the Miss Bradleys' 'Deanery
Guide' :—

'Edward the Confessor's great church was close to his own palace. It
was designed by him for his own burial-place. He was interred before the
altar within a few days of its consecration. From that moment Norman
kings, monks, clergy, and the English people, vied with each other in
honouring his name. William the Conqueror based his claim to the Crown
on an alleged gift of the King, who had long lived in exile in Normandy.
To the monks he was dear not only from his munificent donations, but as
being in life and character almost one of themselves. The Commons of
England, groaning under a foreign yoke, looked back to the peaceful reign
of the pious and gentle Confessor, the last king of the old English stock,
as to a golden age.'

There was thus a universal veneration, on the part of friends and enemies, for Edward 'the Confessor'; and men who could agree about nothing else, could agree in respect for the builder of Westminster Abbey.

It is hardly possible to doubt that before Edward's time the church of the Abbey was the parish church of the neighbourhood. But this did not suit either the monks or the people. The monks did not like the people to crowd into their church, the people wanted a parson of their own. At first the people were permitted to worship in the north aisle of the nave, but very soon St. Margaret's was built. It is sometimes asserted that the Confessor himself was the founder of St. Margaret's. There are many difficulties about this view, which it is not necessary to examine here. The church was probably not in existence in 1086, but was certainly built before 1140. The dedication to St. Margaret was a very common one in England at that period.

This building and consecration of a parish church close to one which was chiefly monastic was a very common arrangement at the time. At St. Helen's, Bishopsgate, a second aisle was built for the parishioners. At St. Albans the Church of St. Andrew was built on the northern side of the Abbey Church, and was only pulled down when, at the Reformation, the parish gained, or regained, the monastic church. At St. Margaret's the case was different. The church of the Abbey was made collegiate, and the parishioners had to remain in their own. The outlines of St. Margaret's, as we now see them, are not very lovely. Repeated restorations have left very little that is old. But it serves as an admirable foil to the great church beside it. It is supposed by long tradition and custom to be in the special care and keeping of the House of Commons, and it certainly is the church of the parish in

Dunster Abbey and Stafford
G4

which the Lower House sits, the House of Lords being in the parish of St. John's. The Commons have made frequent grants for the repair of St. Margaret's. As there is a record of its having been re-dedicated in 1555 by Cardinal Pole, we may safely attribute its present appearance to a rebuilding shortly before that date.

The parish of St. Margaret constituted the principal manor of the Lord Abbot. It was of immense extent, stretching eastward to the walls of the distant city, and northward to the great highway which we call Oxford Street. Its gradual disintegration and separation into the minor parishes is a history in itself. St. Bride's, St. Dunstan's, St. Clement's, St. Mary's, St. Anne's, St. Paul's, St. Martin's, St. James's, St. George's, and St. John's had all been taken out of it before the beginning of this century. And even while the Abbey was in existence and in full working order the manor was encroached upon by the City, and the whole great Ward of Farringdon Without was taken from the Abbot, as well as the little manor of the Savoy.

Westward he had Ebury, or Eybury, close to Westminster, a manor whose name suggests that there was a 'bury,' or mansion-house, on it. Further west still was Chelsea, which in the fourteenth century the Abbot obtained by lease, but could not keep. More to the northward was Hyde. Like Ebury, it was part of the gift of Geoffrey Mandeville, shortly after the Conquest, and comprised the land which lay between the Tyburn on the east and the Westbourne on the west. Beyond the Westbourne, again, there was an outlying estate, Neat, or Neyte, on which, near the town of Kensington, was a dwelling-house much frequented by the abbots. It is now Kensington Palace.

In addition to these suburban manors the Abbey had also

Staines, Sunbury, Shepperton (by the gift of Ulf, the portreeve of London), Greenford, Hanwell, Cowley, Kingsbury, and Hendon. All these manors are in Middlesex, and there were other holdings in more distant counties. It is curious that Paddington should be left unmentioned by Domesday, for not only did it belong to the Abbey from the days of King Edgar, but it went at the Reformation to the shortlived bishopric of Westminster, and has ever since formed part of the estates of the See of London. Westbourne, which must have been included in King Edgar's gift with Paddington, was taken from 'St. Peter' by Henry.VIII., but soon restored, and now belongs to the Dean and Chapter, like Westminster itself.

With these great endowments it may easily be believed that the Lord Abbot and his monks, especially those of them who held official positions, were very great folk in the realm. The Abbey buildings grew apace with their inhabitants. Early in the thirteenth century the young king, Henry III., began to show great veneration for the memory of his canonised predecessor. In 1220 a new Lady Chapel was added to the church eastward; but a little later the King conceived the idea of further honouring St. Edward, by pulling down every vestige of the church he had built on so splendid a scale, and of rebuilding it on a still more splendid scale and in a style wholly different from the plain, solid Norman of Edward's church. The saint whom Edward venerated was Peter the Apostle. He is now thrust into the background, and the great central feature of the new church is the Chapel of St. Edward, immediately behind the high altar, with his shrine, surrounded by a ring of buried kings and queens.

One never enters the Abbey Church without a thrill of admiration for the daring genius who raised those lofty vaults. That they were the first of their kind in England is almost certain, but the name of their designer does not seem to have been preserved. It is more likely that he was an Englishman who had studied in France than that he was a Frenchman. Certain it is that though the plan, if not all the design, is purely French, the arrangement of the chapels being in fact peculiar to Westminster amongst English churches, the workmanship is very superior to that in any contemporary building on the Continent. At St. Paul's the tall, plain gable, with its beautiful rose window, which looked out eastward upon Cheap, was contemporary with the semi-circular church at Westminster and its cluster of chapels. It was the great building age of England, that thirteenth century, and to it we owe, in addition to so many fine works long ago destroyed, the great Cathedral of Salisbury, the most perfect building, next to the Parthenon, ever designed; Whitby, whose noble skeleton still looks out over the Northern Sea; Fountains and Rievaulx, and the noble transept of York, with its tall sister lancets; and many another, great or small, including the exquisitely-proportioned little church at Climping, which is to Salisbury what St. Stephen's, Walbrook, is to St. Paul's. These and others survived intact till our own day, but have all suffered of late years, and none more than Westminster, at the hands of ignorant or vain architects, under the name of 'restoration.'

When Henry had completed his new church as far as the crossing of the transepts and the nave, he held a great consecration festival, at which nothing was omitted that could mark his reverence for St. Edward. It is said—I do not know on what authority—that St. Edward's Chapel owes its elevation above the surrounding chapels to a mound of earth which the King caused to be brought in ships from the Holy Land. The Translation of St. Edward rather than St. Peter's Day (29th June) became the greatest of the Abbey feasts; and by

Cloyster
Garth

Herbert Railton

way of marking it yet more distinctly, and connecting with
it a pecuniary advantage, he insisted on opening a fair at
Westminster, in contravention of the charter of the City of
London; and the citizens, as their chronicler dryly remarks,
'not compelled, and yet as though compelled,' had to resort
to it, their own shops being closed.   About the same time he
endeavoured to obtain from the City the freedom he had
granted to the Abbey by an illegal charter; but the citizens
of those days stoutly defended the rights they had acquired
as Sheriffs in Middlesex, and could never be got to consent
to Henry's innovations.   Nevertheless, the Abbot was exempt
from any interference of the Bishop of London, and to this
day the Dean and Chapter continue to assert for themselves
and their church the same independence.   For a short time
it was a Cathedral, and Westminster was made a city, though
it never had a municipality; but the bishopric only lasted ten
years, from 1540 to 1550, and the church is strictly described
as a royal chapel under the name of the Collegiate Church of
St. Peter.

When Henry pulled down that part of the church in which
the body of St. Edward had been enshrined on his canonisation by Henry II., he removed the holy relics to his palace
hard by.   Peter, a Roman, who had brought the materials
with him, built the new shrine of precious mosaic, of which
some remnants are still to be seen.   On the 13th of October,
1269, the work was complete.   Two kings, Henry himself
and his brother the King of the Romans, with the King's
four sons, carried the saint's coffin in solemn procession from
the palace to the new church, and the feast of the translation
was kept as a day quite as holy as the regular 'Saint's Day,'
the 16th of March.

The chief structural alterations which have taken place

since Henry III. completed the eastern part of his church are the erection of the curious chantry of Henry V., the removal of the Lady Chapel, and the substitution for it of the splendid Chapel of Henry VII., and the addition of the western towers. It has been ascertained that the Lady Chapel of Henry III. extended as far east as that of Henry VII., but had no aisles. Standing at the steps which lead into the Chapel we may see side by side specimens of three different architectural periods, namely, those of Henry III., Henry V., and Henry VII.

The nave was not finished for many years after the death of Henry III. His son, Edward I., called after the saint, carried the work only as far as the western end of the choir : at least this was the opinion of the late Mr. Grahame. Sir Gilbert Scott, however, attributes five bays to Edward I., which would bring his work as far west as the spot in which Sir Gilbert himself was buried in 1878. That some kind of spire, or a *flèche*, was intended for the crossing of the choir, nave, and transepts is very certain, and Wren perceived the want. His design was not, however, carried into execution, and the church retains to this day an unfinished look. The western towers were built when Wren had reached extreme old age, and are not worthy of the designer of St. Mary Aldermary, or St. Alban, Wood Street. In fact, they are generally attributed to Hawksmoor, one of Wren's pupils.

Once we read of the whole body of the monks removing, or being removed, to other quarters. Abbot Herbert, some time before 1240, had founded, with the approval of the Bishops, a little nunnery at Kilburn, dedicated to St. John the Baptist, whence, rather than from the knights of Clerkenwell, we have the modern St. John's Wood. It was situated on the southern slope of Hampstead, which belonged, as we have seen, to the

Abbey, and Herbert endowed it with a little estate, adjoining another Westminster manor, Neyte, namely, what we call Kensington Gore. Hither one day in the fourteenth century the Abbot and all the monks fled, because some one had prophesied that a great tide would come up the Thames and overwhelm the Abbey and all that belonged to it. But the tide came and went as usual, and the monks soon returned to their old quarters.

Another removal was of a forcible character. Edward I. stored in his Treasury, near the Chapter-house of the Abbey, a large sum of money for the expenses of his Scottish campaign in 1303. In April or May it was discovered that the Treasury had been broken into and a large sum stolen. The King ordered an investigation, the Abbot and eighty monks were conveyed to the Tower, and eventually the thieves were found. The Sub-Prior, and the Sacrist, and a foreign merchant, Podelicote by name, were among the guilty. The late Mr. Burtt, of the Record Office, discovered a full account of the robbery and its consequences, and published it in his contribution to the volume of 'Gleanings' already mentioned. Jurors were summoned wherever any part of the objects stolen was found. 'They were summoned, not as now from their ignorance, but for their knowledge of the facts.' In every ward of the City, and in many places in all the 'home counties,' evidence was collected. What chiefly concerned the Abbey was the conduct of the Sacrist, the Sub-Prior, and certain other monks, who had been seen to go in and out, early and late, carrying things. One Alexander, of Pershore, a monk, was seen entering a boat at the King's Bridge, a landing-place very near the western end of Westminster Bridge, carrying great panniers covered with leather. Another monk was suspected because he took to dressing himself magnifi-

THE DEANERY.

D

cently, and boasted that he could buy a whole town if he
pleased. Another, who had sowed the burial-ground round
the Chapter House with hemp, in order to conceal stolen
objects in the thick foliage, obliterated the tracks of the
robbers. The value of the things lost amounted to about two
millions of money, according to Mr. Burtt. Podelicote, when
he was caught, had 2200*l.* worth in his possession ; but the
thieves evidently had great trouble to get rid of the cups, rings,
chains, jewels, and miscellaneous articles, and many goldsmiths
and jewellers in the City and elsewhere were implicated. The
hemp-sowing shows with what deliberation and long preparation
the whole plot had been conceived and executed. An immense
quantity of plunder was eventually recovered, and, no doubt,
though the records do not mention the fact, the Sacrist, the
Sub-Prior, and Podelicote, if not many more, suffered the last
penalty of the law for their crime. The door adjoining the
entrance to the Chapter House, which led to the violated
Treasury, was covered with the skins of the robbers as a terror
to future monks, and a fragment is still in its place. 'The
same terrible lining,' says Dean Stanley, 'is also affixed to the
door of the Sacristy in the south transept of the Abbey,' usually
called the Chapel of St. Blaise.

· The domestic buildings of the Abbey remained till the end
in great part as they were left by the Confessor, but Abbot
Litlington rebuilt the west and south walks of the cloister
between 1376 and 1386, the Abbot's residence, now the
Deanery, the east side of Dean's Yard, and the Refectory, the
wall of which can be seen in the garden of Ashburnham House,
now appropriated by Westminster School. The work of
Litlington is in a curious transitional style, and can hardly be
mistaken, though it has been cruelly maltreated by restorers of
late years. He had unlimited means at his disposal, for

Cardinal Langham, who had once been Abbot, made the Abbey his residuary legatee, leaving what would be nearly 200,000*l.* in our money. The Perpendicular style had not quite come in, though William of Wykeham was employing it at Oxford and Windsor. But Litlington was probably his own architect, and to him, no doubt, we owe what is now called the Queen's Scholars' Hall, the chambers called 'Jerusalem' and 'Jericho,' probably from paintings of those places which adorned them, and much besides.

The last abbot was Boston, the first dean was Benson; but Abbot Boston and Dean Benson were one and the same individual. It must have been a bitter thing to descend from the position of a peer of Parliament, controlling an income which would amount in our day to over 60,000*l.* a year, to leave the palatial deanery, and live in a small house adapted from the Misericorde of the dissolved Abbey. But Abbot Boston had been specially selected by Cromwell for the work he was intended to do, and we cannot greatly pity him, though it is stated that he repented him when it was too late, and died of 'taking care.' He did his best to save some of the Abbey estates for the new Deanery and the Chapter, with partial success. The Abbot's house was given to the newly-created Bishop of Westminster, but Thurlby, the first bishop, was also the last. The house was next given to Lord Wentworth, and when Feckenham, under Queen Mary, was commissioned to restore the ancient Abbey, he effected an exchange, and obtained the old house by the sacrifice of a manor. Only seventeen monks were left of the old seventy at the suppression, and Feckenham, who was called after his birthplace in Suffolk, but whose real name was Howman, brought in fourteen. He was not in office a year, and can hardly be reckoned one of the old succession, though in the first year of Queen Elizabeth he

took his seat in Parliament as Lord Abbot. But in 1560 he
was formally deprived, and William Bill became dean, and was
allowed the old house, which has ever since been the deanery.
He did not long survive, and in 1561 was succeeded by the
great Dean Goodman, a Welshman by birth, whom his successor,
Dean Stanley, well describes as 'the real founder of the present
establishment.'

IV

CORONATIONS

The first Coronation—Harold II.—William the Conqueror—His Crown—
Its Destruction—The Service—The 'Recognition' and its Meaning—
The Coronation of Queens—The Coronation of Queen Victoria—The
Anointing—Charles II.—The Spurs—The Sword—King Edward's
Chair—The Stone—Its Legendary History—Its Geological Character
—Anecdotes of Coronations.

THE first coronation in Westminster Abbey must have been
that of Harold, beside the newly-made grave of his
predecessor, Edward. It is only, however, by a process of
elaborate deduction that Mr. Freeman comes to the conclusion
that this was the place. Edward had been crowned at
Winchester. Several of his immediate predecessors had been
crowned in London at St. Paul's, and Kingston-upon-Thames
was the crowning-place of the old kings. But that Westminster
was the scene of Harold's coronation is as certain as anything
can be of which we have not actual contemporary evidence.
Aldred, archbishop of York, officiated, and not Stigand,
archbishop of Canterbury, as mistakenly represented on the
Bayeux tapestry; and the ceremony followed immediately the
burial of Edward, on the feast of the Epiphany, January the
6th, 1066. It was a Friday. Perhaps the death of Harold,
nine months later, at Hastings, and the misfortunes which fell
upon his countrymen, may have had something to do with the

establishment of the very ancient popular superstition that 'Friday is an unlucky day.'

It has been reasonably pointed out that the coronation of Harold's conqueror in Westminster is a portion of the evidence as to the place of Harold's own coronation. A year had not elapsed. It was on Christmas Day in 1066, and again Aldred was the officiating prelate. A new crown was made for the ceremony. Perhaps this was the crown which was called in after ages the Confessor's, and which was broken up under the Commonwealth; and still more likely it was the Crown kept at Westminster and described in the Parliamentary inventory ('Archaeologia,' xv. 288), in which we have a list of 'that part of the Regalia which are now removed from Westminster to the Tower Jewell-house.' First we have 'Queene Edith's crowne, formerly thought to be of massy gould, but upon triall found to be of silver gilt, enriched with garnetts, foule pearle, saphires, and some odd stones, per ounce 50 ounces ½ valued at £16 0 0.' It need hardly be mentioned that the wife of the Confessor was not called queen, and was certainly never crowned.

The silver-gilt crown called after the Lady Edith must have been made at a later period. Next we come to 'King Alfred's crowne, of gould wyerworke, sett with slight stones and 2 little bells.' This weighed 79 ounces and was valued at 248*l*. 10*s*. What would not one give for even a momentary glance at it? But, alas! we read on another page of the inventory, 'the formention'd crownes, since the inventory was taken, are according to ord^r of Parlam^t, totallie broken and defaced.' No doubt the crown of King Alfred, with its 'gould wyerworke' and its bells shared the same fate.

While William was being crowned within the Abbey, his soldiers, alarmed at the cheers of the congregation instead of

THE NAVE.

rushing in to his help, if they thought he was attacked, 'hastened, with the strange instinct of their nation, to set fire to the buildings around the minster.' The spectators of the sacred rites rushed forth to save their houses. The King was left with the Archbishop and the monks, while the flames roared without, and the noise of the tumult could be heard loud above the anthems and psalms. William, it is said, trembled ; but the Archbishop completed the ceremony, and administered the oath which had been specially drawn up to meet the case of a foreign king. During the Norman period the oath was administered before the 'recognition,' which appears to have been a survival of the old form of election. When the King had engaged and sworn to do justly by the people, they were asked if they would have him to reign over them ; and it may well have been their vociferous answer, as if to reassert their ancient rights even before the great conqueror himself, that alarmed the Norman guards. At the coronation of Charles II., and probably long before, this 'recognition' preceded the oath, and, in fact, had evidently lost its meaning. At the last few coronations the voice of the people of England, electing their sovereign by acclamation, has only been heard in 'the shouts of Westminster scholars, from their recognised seats in the Abbey.' But since the reign of Henry VIII. its significance has been lost and its place altered.

The ceremony, unknown before, of the coronation of a queen, took place in the Abbey in May, 1068. As the contemporary chronicler, Ordericus, notes, Matilda was 'hallowed to queen' (cwene). The ceremony took place on Whit Sunday, and Aldred again officiated. The wife of Edward, Eadgyth, or Edith, is sometimes called 'Cwene,' but generally 'the Lady,' and the King's mother, the widow of Cnut, 'the Old Lady.'

The ritual still employed is of extreme antiquity. It is usually described as that of King Ethelred. But it is probably still older. A contemporary account of Ethelred's coronation is preserved among the Cottonian manuscripts, and demonstrates that some of the most eloquent passages in the modern office were then already in use. It is interesting to see, in a volume now before me, 'The Form and Order of the Service that is to be performed, and of the Ceremonies that are to be observed, in the coronation of Her Majesty Queen Victoria, in the Abbey Church of St. Peter, Westminster, on Thursday, the 28th of June, 1838,' that certain of the prayers are the same as those which were said at the coronation of Ethelred, nearly nine hundred years ago, and which had probably come down to his day from a remote period. The volume is bound in purple, and has the arms of Lord Clare on the sides, so that it may have been actually used in the Abbey.

The coronation may be said to consist of three principal parts : the oath, the unction, and the actual crowning. Before the time of Henry VIII. the 'recognition,' or 'election,' would have made a fourth. We have still, however, the anointing. Among the numerous gold objects in the ancient regalia only the bowl of the anointing spoon survives, fitted to a handle of the time of Charles II. It seems to date from the thirteenth century, and was probably made for Henry III. A vessel in the shape of a bird contains the oil. Whether the bird is a dove, a pelican, or an eagle, I must leave any one who has seen it in the Tower to decide for himself. Personally, I think it is a dove, or, to speak more accurately, is intended to represent a dove ; but the goldsmith who made it was anxious to make as near a copy from memory of the old *Ampulla* as he could, with this questionable result. The preparation and consecration of the sacred oil is a duty formerly performed by the Abbot of Westminster and his monks, and it still devolves on the Dean and his Canons, who have the privilege of standing with the Bishops during the ceremonial. The oil used to be poured over the King's head and shoulders, and left to dry, not being wiped off. Meanwhile for six days the King was covered with a white linen coif. In the account left us by Sir Edward Walker, the Garter King of Arms, who was present at the coronation of Charles II., we read that the Archbishop (Juxon), 'who by reason of his infirmity had until that time reposed himself in St. Edward's Chapel, came out,' wearing a rich ancient cope; and the King coming up to the altar was disrobed by the Lord Great Chamberlain, hose and sandals being put on his feet. The ribbons which closed his crimson satin coat were untied and the shirt underneath was opened. The 'Ampull,' with the oil and the spoon, were brought from the altar, the Dean holding the vessel and pouring the oil into the spoon. Then, with various prayers and sentences said or sung, the King's hands were first anointed, then the oil was poured on his breast, between his shoulders, on both shoulders, on his elbows, and, lastly, on the crown of his head, 'which donne, the Deane closed the ribbands.' A coif of lawn was then placed over the King's head by the Archbishop. At the coronation of Queen Victoria this is the official account of the anointing :—

'The Queen will then sit down in King Edward's Chair, placed in the midst of the area over against the altar, with a faldstool before it wherein she is to be anointed. Four Knights of the Garter hold over her a rich pall of silk or cloth of gold; the anthem being concluded, the Dean of Westminster, taking the ampulla and spoon from off the altar, holdeth them ready, pouring some of the holy oil into the spoon, and with it the Archbishop anointeth the Queen in the form of a cross on the crown of the head and on the palms of both hands, saying, "Be thou anointed with holy oil, as kings, priests, and prophets were anointed."'

Another curious ceremony is the presentation of the spurs. This is supposed, if the King is not already a knight, to make him one. The Queen must be held to be a knight, as she is able to confer knighthood; but it may be said that her own

Tombs in the Sacrarium

Aveline of Lancaster   Aymer de Valence   Edmund Crouchback.

knighthood dates from the presentation of the golden spurs, directly after the anointing. The spurs used are among the regalia in the Tower, and are placed on the altar before the ceremony. At the coronation of Charles II. they were put on the King's heels by the Lord Chamberlain, kneeling. Of

George III. we read that the spurs 'were only applied to the King's heel, and immediately afterwards returned to the altar.' At the coronation of George IV. they were presented only and returned to the altar. Queen Victoria also received and returned them, as well as the sword of state, which was returned, as on former occasions, by the sovereign herself :—

'Then the Queen, rising up and going to the altar, offers the sword there in the scabbard, delivering it to the Archbishop, who places it on the altar; the Queen then returns and sits down in King Edward's Chair, and the Lord who first received the sword offereth the price of it, and having thus redeemed it, receiveth it from off the altar by the Dean of Westminster, and draweth it out of the scabbard, and carries it naked before her Majesty during the rest of the solemnity.'

The coronation takes place while the Sovereign is seated in King Edward's Chair. It must have been specially constructed for the reception of the famous stone which Edward I. brought from Scotland in 1296, and has been constantly used at coronations ever since, the last time it was brought out from the chapel where it stands being for the Jubilee Thanksgiving Service, when the Queen sat in it during the ceremonial.

The history of the stone is briefly as follows :—A Greek brought from Egypt into Spain, in or about the time of Moses, the identical stone from Bethel on which the patriarch Jacob laid his head when he saw the heavenly ladder. In the eighth century B.C. King Simon Brech took it to Ireland. Four hundred years later it was transferred to Scotland by King Fergus, more than three centuries B.C. Such is the legendary history of the stone on which unquestionably a number of Scottish kings were crowned at Scone. In 1296 it was removed by Edward I. to Westminster, and mention is made of it in lists of things belonging to the Abbey

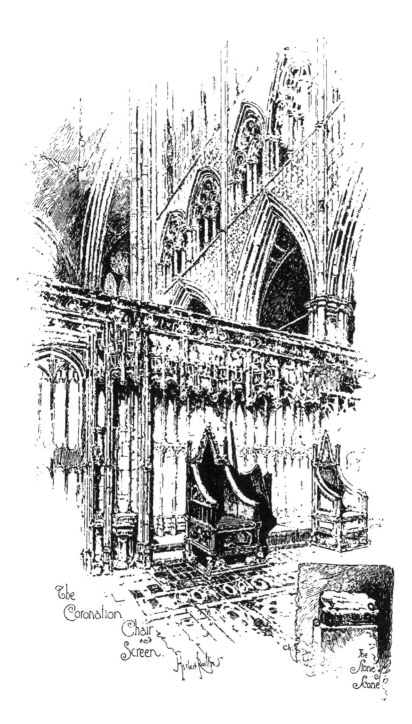

The
Coronation
Chair
and
Screen.

Herbert Railton

ch.

The
Stone
Scone

as 'una petra magna super quam reges Scociae solebant coronari.' In 1865 Dean Stanley asked Professor Ramsay, the geologist, to examine the stone, and he gives the result in his 'Memorials.' It is 'of a dull reddish or purplish sandstone,' of the kind masons call 'freestone'; and he is inclined to attribute its origin to the neighbourhood of Dunstaffnage, whence it went, as is known, to Scone. But the Professor is mistaken when he says there is no sandstone of the same character in Egypt, for one of the most celebrated statues in the world, the so-called *Vocal Memnon*, is made of it.

Horace Walpole was in Westminster Hall when George III. and Queen Charlotte were crowned. The sword of state, he says, was forgotten, and the Lord Mayor's was borrowed for the occasion. 'By a childish compliment,' the Hall was not lighted up until the King's arrival, and as it was late in the afternoon (22nd of September, 1761), the Hall was dark, and the procession, with the Knights of the Bath wearing plumes, was 'like a funeral.'

An interval of nearly sixty years elapsed before George IV. came to Westminster for his coronation, and the pageant on that occasion exceeded everything that had been seen by those present. Nothing was omitted that could add to the solemnity and magnificence of the show.

The King's bed was removed from Carlton House to the Speaker's official residence, and he slept on the night of the 18th, we are told, 'in the Tapestry-room, looking out over the Thames,' the last time the old Palace was inhabited by a king. The King arrived at half-past eight and supped with his host. The next morning was as fine as the day which saw the Queen's Jubilee in 1887. The King entered Westminster Hall at ten, and already 'appeared to be somewhat fatigued.' He, however, himself superintended the arrangements, and gave each of the grand functionaries the piece of the regalia which he was to carry. The Dean and Chapter had brought them all over from the Abbey. When he handed the crown to Lord Anglesey he graciously dispensed with his walking backwards in retiring, as the Marquis had lost a leg at Waterloo six years before. The banquet in the Hall took place at five, the procession having only left the Abbey at four. When all was over the King returned to Carlton House in the twilight of the summer evening.

The effect of this pageant on the art and literature of the succeeding period was immense. The revival of a mediaeval ceremonial necessitated the revival of mediaeval art. Heraldry and architecture received the strongest stimulus. Historical novels became the rage; and, no doubt, a great deal of the hold which the Gothic style took on the building genius of the day must be ascribed to the coronation of George IV.

V

THE CONFESSOR'S CHAPEL

Incongruity of the First Monuments—A Modest Proposal—Henry III.—
Queen Eleanor—Are they Portraits?—William Torel—Queen Philippa
—Edward III.—Richard II. and Queen Anne—Thomas of Woodstock
—The Lady Edith—Queen Matilda—Edward I.—'Pactum Serva'—
Examination of his body in 1774—Monument of Henry V.—The
Reredos —Funeral of Henry V.

IT is well worth while to point out that the first monuments
erected in the Church of Henry III. were in an incongruous style.   While the 'great Gothic revival' and its destructive
companion, 'restoration,' were all-powerful, it was seriously
proposed to take out of the Abbey everything that was not
judged to be strictly in what Pugin used to call 'the Christian
Pointed Style.'   But nobody, so far at least as I am aware,
ever remarked that the first monuments to be condemned on
this principle would have been the shrine of Edward the
Confessor, the tomb of Henry III., and the magnificent
monument of Henry VII.   Incongruity among things beautiful
in themselves is the very first element of the picturesque.   As
it is, though Westminster Abbey has suffered much, and is
suffering more, at the hands of the modern 'restorer,' its
delightful want of uniformity is not, and can hardly ever be,
overcome.   Besides sweeping out all the monuments erected
between the reigns of Queen Elizabeth and Queen Victoria,

THE CONFESSOR'S CHAPEL.

we should have to take down the banners of the knights in the
chapel of Henry VII., the statues of St. Peter and St. Paul,
the tapestry, the pulpits in the choir and in the nave—but it is
not worth while to go on : the task would be impossible, though
it might have been undertaken by one of the modest architects
of the generation which ruined so many other buildings—
Salisbury, for example, and Hereford, the Temple, St. Albans,
and hundreds of parish churches.

The learned in such matters assert that the oldest statues
are not portraits, but conventional representations of kings, and
queens, and nobles.   I confess to a strong feeling of reluctance
in accepting this verdict.   If the beautiful Eleanor of Castile
was not like the marvellous figure on her tomb, she cannot at
least have been very different.   As to her father-in-law, Henry
III., perhaps, as all contemporary accounts make him an ugly
little man, with a squint, the portrait may be flattered ; but
that it is more or less a portrait, however much idealised,
would seem certain, if only because of the way in which the
features answer to what we know was the character of the
King.   Handsome as they are, we think we can detect in them
the weakness, cowardice, falsehood, treachery, and tyranny
which characterised Henry III., as well as the magnificence,
the taste for art, the polish, and the courtliness which made
him the stranger's friend.   Perhaps the effigy does not bear me
out in this opinion, and it may be well, lest the reader be
led astray, to quote the opinion of an expert.   The late Mr.
William Burges, R.A., says of the effigy of Henry III.: 'The
face is purely conventional and such as we shall see in
nearly every effigy of the period.'   He praises the hands, but
says they are not 'cast from the life, like those of Torregiano's
effigy of the Countess of Richmond.'   Of Queen Eleanor's
effigy he says :—

SOUTH AISLE OF THE CHOIR.

'On the top of the Purbeck tomb is the *chef d'œuvre* of William Torel, goldsmith and citizen of London, and who, for the honour of our country, appears to have nothing whatever to do with the Italian family of Torelli, as the name Torel occurs in documents from the time of the Confessor down to the said William : in fact, the attempts of various art critics to prove that the artist of this beautiful figure was an Italian are perfectly inexplicable ; for if we look at the contemporary Italian work at Pisa and elsewhere, we shall find that the English and French, so far from being behind the Italians in the thirteenth century, were, if anything, in advance of them. On examining the statue we discover the same conventionalities as we see in that of Henry III. Thus, the line of the lower eyelid is straight, the *alve* of the nose are small (the nose in this instance is straight) ; there is not much drawing in the mouth, but the middle line goes down a little at either end, and the hair flows down the back in very strong wavy lines. Now Eleanor at the time of her death was over forty years of age, and had had several children ; it is therefore most improbable that this can be a portrait-statue, and, to a certain degree, we are the gainers ; for however curious it would have been to have seen the real likenesses of Henry III. and of Eleanor, it is still more so to have the ideal beauty of one of the great periods of art handed down to us in enduring brass.'

The opinions of Mr. Burges on a matter of this kind will, of course, have great weight, especially with those of us who knew him and recognised his extraordinary critical abilities. It should, however, be stated, on the other side, that there is no inherent impossibility in the opposite view. Burges makes a point of the Queen's age at the time of her death. But could we not, in England, find a beautiful princess, whose children are grown up, and to whose face, so far, no sculptor has yet been able to do justice? Queen Eleanor's forty years can have nothing to do with the portraiture question.

The lower part of the tomb is simply ornamented with shields in low relief. It was the work of Richard of Crundale, who also made the last of the 'Eleanor Crosses,' that erected at Charing. A smith, named Thomas, at Leighton Beaudesert (Buzzard), made the wrought-iron gratings, for which he received 13*l.*—an immense sum in those days. For gilding the statue, Flemish coin was bought—a curious illustration of the meaning of our modern word 'sterling,' or Esterling.

The tomb of Philippa, queen of Edward III., is in a position on the south-east side of the chapel, corresponding to that of Queen Eleanor on the north-east. In the stout effigy which surmounts this monument there can be no doubt of the intention of the artist to make a likeness. Hawkin of Liége has, in fact, almost fallen into caricature.

'The effigy,' says Mr. Burges, 'is probably the first one in Westminster Abbey which has any claims to be considered a portrait. Some parts, such as the head-dress, have been elaborately coloured and gilt.' The portly form and round buxom face of the Queen are well known. The monument is most elaborate, but has suffered much from the later building of the chantry of Henry V. and from the depredations of thieves.

Immediately to the west of Queen Philippa's tomb is that of her husband, Edward III. He is represented as he was, no doubt, in later life—a venerable man, with a long flowing beard. 'The gilt-bronze effigy is remarkable as having connected with it the tradition that the features have been cast from a mould taken after death.'

Next to Edward III., westward, is the larger monument of his grandson, Richard II., who had it made in his own lifetime. It bears the two figures of Richard himself and his first wife, Anne of Bohemia. They were made by Nicholas Broker and Godfrey Prest, London coppersmiths, and are finished in the most elaborate manner—the heraldic decorations alone being worthy of hours of study. The Queen died in 1394, and the tomb was finished in 1397. In 1399 Richard was deposed, and resigned the crown to Henry IV. The canopy over the figures still remains, and shows the remains of painting and gilding. It was decorated by John Haxey, who is believed also to have painted the portrait of Richard which Mr. George Scharff and Mr. Richmond recently cleaned, with the assistance of Mr. Merritt.

The effigies are made up of several separate pieces fitted together; but the hands of the King and Queen, which were clasped together, have been stolen. This display of affection was specially arranged by Richard to show his affection for his wife. She died at Sheen, which Henry VII. re-named Richmond in 1394, and it would seem as if Richard lost any powers of mind he had ever possessed in his extravagant grief. He had the palace in which she died razed to the ground. On the day of the funeral he behaved like a man beside himself, and violently assaulted one of the lords in the Abbey.

The other interments within St. Edward's Chapel are very few in number. The body of the Lady Eadgyth, or Edith, the widow of the Confessor, was, after some migrations, buried on the north side of the shrine, at the foot of the monument of Henry III. She, like Bishop Waltham, is one of the few persons not of royal blood known to have been buried in this chapel: the daughter of Earl Godwin, though she was the sister of Harold, could boast of no very illustrious lineage. At the opposite side of the shrine lies Queen Matilda, the Scottish Princess, the wife of Henry I., who died in 1118. She was the daughter of Malcolm, king of Scotland, by Margaret, the sister of Edgar the Atheling, one of the last scions of the old Saxon stock. Like the companion 'queen' on the north side of the shrine, she bore the ancient English name of Eadgyth, and was living with her aunt the Abbess of Wilton, when the King sought her out. As she had plenty of brothers and sisters, she cannot

Tomb of Richard II.

in any sense be called the heiress of Alfred; but she was a
princess of the old house, and her marriage with Henry I.,
when she changed her name to Matilda, or Maud, was very
popular with Henry's English subjects. Two small princesses
are also buried here, namely, Margaret of York, fifth daughter
of Edward IV., and Elizabeth, daughter of Henry VII.
Roger of Wendover, bishop of Rochester under Henry III.,
is said to have been buried near his master, but no memorial
is extant. Nor is there any monument of Richard Courtenay,
bishop of Norwich, who accompanied his kinsman, Henry V.,
in his French campaign, and died of dysentery at the siege
of Harfleur, in 1415, before the victory of Agincourt. An
infant son of Richard III. is also said to have been laid
in this chapel; and among the treasures of the shrine of
St. Edward was reckoned a golden vase, which contained
the heart of Henry 'of Almain,' a nephew of Henry III.,
whose murder at Viterbo, by the sons of Simon Montfort,
is commemorated by Dante in the 'Inferno.'

We now reach the plainest, but in many respects the most
remarkable, of these royal tombs. The first object which
catches the eye as we ascend to the level of the chapel is
the simple box-like coffin of stone which contains the body
of Edward I. It has often been remarked that monuments
are as much the memorials of those who make them as of
those for whom they are made. In the splendid tomb of
Henry III., with its cunning mosaic, its ruddy porphyry
inlay, its gilded image, we have a memorial of the filial love
of a good son to a bad father, of the loyalty of an obedient
subject to an unscrupulous king. In the delicate tracery,
the exquisite carving, the lovely figure of Queen Eleanor,
we have the monument of Edward's life-long devotion to the
wife whose memory is perhaps as widely kept alive as that

of any queen-consort who has ever shared the throne of an English king. The Eleanor crosses are famous, and this tomb is but the last and crowning effort of the royal mourner in his sorrow. For himself there was no monument necessary. The completion of the Abbey—where sleep his father and his wife—that is monument enough for Edward. The five plain Purbeck slabs, with their grim inscription, are a sufficiently magnificent resting-place for 'the greatest of the Plantagenets.' The epitaph, 'Edvardus Primus, malleus Scotorum, hic est. Pactum serva,' has been a puzzle to people who thought it as old as the tomb. But the letters are of the time of Queen Mary I., and were painted up as a part of Feckenham's 'restoration' of the chapel. He placed similar inscriptions on other tombs, with brief moral sentences to eke out the line.

There are several royal warrants relating to the tomb of King Edward, whose body, carefully embalmed, was at intervals taken out of its coffin for the renewal of the cerecloth in which it was wrapped. In 1774 Dean Thomas gave leave to a committee of the Society of Antiquaries to open and examine the tomb. A plain coffin, hollowed out of a block of Purbeck marble, was found within. When it was opened the body was seen wrapped in waxed linen. When this was thrown back the royal corpse was found to be habited in all the trappings of royalty. The face was dark and wasted, as if with long illness, the nose and eyes were sunk, and the chin was beardless. The dress was very magnificent, though ornamented with imitations of jewels. The mantle was of rich crimson satin, fastened on the left shoulder with a magnificent brooch of gilt metal. A copper-gilt sceptre was held between the thumb and two first fingers of the right hand, and a rod, more than five feet long, surmounted

with the figure of a dove, was in the left hand. A crown
of brass-gilt was on the head; but it was remarked that
the workmanship was not equal to that of the sceptre and
rod. No rings were on the fingers, and if they had slipped
off they were not found, as the body was not further disturbed,
and was carefully covered up again, when a measurement
had been made, which showed that Edward's nickname of
Longshanks was well merited. He must have stood, in his
prime, more than six feet two inches in height.

The monument of Henry V., owing to its extraordinary
magnificence, has suffered more than any other in the Chapel
of St. Edward. It can, perhaps, hardly be described as in
the chapel, for though the tomb stands on the utmost eastern
verge of the mound of holy earth, it is separated from its
regal companions by the supports of the chantry or Chapel
of the Annunciation above. It was evidently intended by
the designer of this tomb, that it should not only occupy
the most important place next to that of the shrine itself,
but that it should be the finest of all the royal monuments.
The figure, of oak, was covered with silver plates, and the
head was of solid silver, or, more probably, was a hollow
silver casting. All is gone now but a shapeless, headless
block of wood. The silver plates were stripped off, and
the head stolen, some time in the reign of Henry VIII.
The same fate had already overtaken the golden shrine of
Edward the Confessor, of which Brayley says that 'the
workmanship exceeded the materials.' This chapel and the
tomb of Henry must have been a perfect blaze of colour.
Gilding, silver, precious stones, mosaic, and every other
device known at the time, were employed to add to the
effect. Both the chantry at the east end and the screen
at the west end seem to have been the work of Henry VI.

The screen has been so thoroughly *restored* that very little, if any, of the old work remains. On its western side was the beautiful Renaissance reredos, designed by Inigo Jones, which had previously stood in the private chapel at Whitehall. When that palace was burnt, it was fortunately saved, and was removed to Hampton Court, where, however, it was never set up. In 1706 Queen Anne, apparently at the instance of Sir Christopher Wren, had it taken out of the stores there, and presented it to the Dean and Chapter, to be set up in the Abbey. It must have been a very beautiful structure, not too large, but otherwise something like the reredos recently placed in St. Paul's. What has become of Inigo Jones's beautiful work I do not know. A small fragment is in the triforium.

The funeral of Henry V. was the most imposing function of the kind ever witnessed in England up to that time. He died, apparently of dysentery, at Vincennes, near Paris, on the last day of August, 1422. His funeral at Westminster took place on the 7th of November. 'His three chargers were led up,' says Dean Stanley, 'to the altar, behind the effigy, which lay on the splendid car, accompanied by torches and white-robed priests innumerable.' A service had been held at Notre Dame, in Paris, next at Rouen, and thirdly at St. Paul's. The coffin was placed in an open chariot, whereon also, on a bed covered with crimson silk, was an image of the King made of *cuir bouilli*—leather soaked in hot water to make it pliable, a favourite material for many purposes, such as tilting armour, crests, boxes, and other objects. The image was, of course, coloured, and was clothed in a purple robe edged with ermine, with a crown on the head and a sceptre in the hand. The widowed queen followed a league behind; and the voice of the chanters

was kept up incessantly all the way, masses being celebrated
every morning wherever the procession had halted for the
night.   Fifteen bishops went from London towards Rochester
to meet the procession, and an immense concourse of the
citizens went with them.   The body remained some time
at St. Paul's while the Abbey was prepared for its reception.
From St. Paul's the hearse was drawn by six horses, each
of which bore a different coat-of-arms : St. George, Normandy,
King Arthur, St. Edward, France, and the King's own
'scutcheon of France and England, quarterly.   The chief
mourner was the King of Scotland, James I.   Five hundred
men-at-arms in black, with their lances reversed, must have
presented an imposing appearance, to say nothing of three
hundred more with torches.   The funeral helmet, saddle,
and shield were hung on a cross-beam.   The shield has
lost its heraldry, but it and the saddle and the helmet are
still in their places.   The accounts furnished by the undertaker are extant, and include the helmet, unfortunately for
Dean Stanley's reference to 'the very casque that did affright
the air at Agincourt.'

VI

CHAPEL OF HENRY VII

Chapel of Henry VII.—The Reredos—The Altar—Burial of Henry VII.
—The Tomb—The Building of the Chapel—Torregiano—Margaret,
Countess of Richmond and Derby—Edward VI.—Queen Mary—
Queen Elizabeth—Machyn's Diary—The Royal Vaults.

FROM the tomb of Henry V. under the Chapel of the
Annunciation to the entrance of the Chapel of our
Blessed Lady is but a few steps, yet if we examine the piers
on either side we may trace three distinct architectural
periods.   First, there is the early work of Henry III., who,
it will be remembered, made a Lady Chapel here before
he commenced the rebuilding of the Confessor's church.
Secondly, the next pier shows us the work done when the
body of Henry V. was brought hither from France in 1422.
Lastly, alongside of these two is the first column of the
new and gorgeous structure with which Henry VII. replaced
the Lady Chapel of Henry III.   We ascend gradually and
in comparative darkness, the effect of the gorgeous building
beyond being much enhanced by the gloom of the approach.
The great barred-in tomb of Henry VII. stands just beyond
the altar, but was concealed from view by the lofty reredos
which Torregiano made and adorned with costly marble
inlay and carving, and with a wonderful figure of the Dead

Christ surrounded by angels, all exquisitely modelled in terra-cotta. The broken-up fragments remain in the triforium, for the whole reredos was destroyed by a certain Sir Robert Harlow in 1643. It used to be described as the monument of Edward VI., who was buried under it. Some fragments of the marble altar were identified by Professor Middleton among the Arundel marbles at Oxford, and other pieces in the grave below, and have been restored to the chapel, forming the supports of the new altar.

Henry VII. was buried on the 10th of May, 1509, after a long funeral procession from Richmond, where he died, through the City of London. Measures were at once taken for the construction of the monument. Laurence Ymber was employed to make a design, but the execution was eventually entrusted to the famous Italian sculptor, Torregiano. Ymber seems to have worked with him. He was perhaps the artist who made the strictly Gothic part of the structure, such as 'the grate.' The whole building is always said to have been designed by Sir Reginald Bray, but he can have had no hand in carrying out his plans, as he died within a few months of the laying of the foundation stone in 1503.

In his will Henry gave very careful and special directions concerning his burial, and intended that the body of Henry VI. should also be laid in the new chapel. In a council held at Greenwich the rival claims of Chertsey, where he was first buried, Windsor, where he then lay, and Westminster, where he had selected a place for his tomb, were considered, and Westminster was chosen. The Abbot was charged 500*l.*, equal to at least as many thousands now, and seems actually to have paid it. He probably never saw the money again, but neither did he obtain the body of Henry VI. There seems to be no doubt that it still rests at Windsor; at all events, it was never

HENRY VII.'S CHAPEL.

removed to Westminster, and the scanty respect shown to monuments and memorials under the Tudors and during the Civil War obliterated any marks by which his grave at Windsor could be identified.

Bishop Alcock, of Ely, is sometimes assigned a share in the credit of making the design for the chapel. It is not improbable that he was closely concerned with Bray, but though he was 'master of the King's works,' he can have had nc hand in the actual erection, as he died in 1500, before even the foundation was laid; but, as one of the most accomplished architects of the time, he may well have helped in the drawings and specifications. But the credit is due to a third competitor, the Prior of St. Bartholomew's, in Smithfield, who is mentioned in Henry's will as actually at work. This was Prior Bolton, whose 'device,' a bolt and a tun, are still to be seen in what remains of the great church of his house which he repaired. He, no doubt, was responsible for carrying out the design referred to in the will as a 'plat,' or a 'picture.'

The Harleian Library in the British Museum and the Office of the Rolls in Fetter Lane both contain copies of the 'indenture' made between Henry VII. and the monastery of Westminster as to the religious observances in the chapel, and as to their continuance 'whilst the world shall endure.' Alas for human expectations! Henry VII. probably thought there could not possibly be, or be conceived, an institution more likely to be permanent than the Abbey of Westminster, or more likely to last as long as the world shall endure. Less than fifty years after the death of Henry VII. the last flicker of the tapers at his shrine had died out.

Architecturally speaking, the chapel consists of a nave, two side-aisles, and five smaller apsidal chapels. There is no public entrance but from the interior of the Abbey, but there is a

HENRY VII.'S SHRINE.

F

small workmen's door in the south-eastern turret, by which
access may be had to the south aisle. The vaulting is supported by fourteen buttresses, or turrets, between which are
thirteen windows. Turrets and walls are alike covered with a
lace-like pattern, and every part is enriched with minute tracery,
and hundreds, if not thousands, of roses, portcullises, fleurs-de-
lis, lions, dragons, and greyhounds. But the roof is the great
glory of the chapel. It is reasonable to suppose that it
was built by the same men who made that of the very similar,
but less elaborate, choir at St. George's at Windsor, where
John Hylmer and William Vertue were the chief masons.

The tomb and the effigies of the King and Queen upon it
are in a style wholly different from that of the grate or of the
chapel. They are, in fact, purely Italian, and, as I have
remarked already, remind us that the Romanesque, whose
last dying efforts are to be seen in the shrine of the Confessor
and the tomb of Henry III., has now revived and come
back to us from Italy in the work of Torregiano. The
statues excited the deepest admiration. The proportions,
the anatomy, the muscular modelling, were seen here for
the first time. Bacon speaks of the tomb as 'one of the
stateliest and daintiest monuments of Europe.' Mr. Burges,
who could not be accused of any special partiality for the
Renaissance, says it 'will bear comparison with any other
work of the time, either in Italy or elsewhere.'

Of Torregiano's work we have two other acknowledged
examples, at least; the monument of the Countess of Derby,
the mother of Henry VII., in bronze, which is in the south
aisle of the chapel, and the little known but most interesting
tomb of John Young, dean of York, and Master of the Rolls,
which still exists in the Rolls Chapel. The tomb of Henry VII.
is in a later style than either of these, having probably been

One Bay.
Henry VII
Chapel.

finished after Torregiano's visit to Florence in 1518. The
tomb is fairly intact, though the crowns of the King and
Queen, and some other removable ornaments, as well as the
covering of the chantry itself, have disappeared. The most
beautiful feature of the design is perhaps the little angels at
the corners. They seem to have scarcely alighted, and to
be ready to take flight again in a moment.

The tomb of the Lady Margaret has in it qualities even
superior to those of the tomb of Henry VII. No such
wonderful hands have ever been modelled as that lean, old,
wrinkled, withered pair. One feels that the very veins on it
are portraits. As for the face, it is hardly as good as the
hands, yet one reads in it the goodness of disposition, the
benevolence and liberality of the King's mother, whose name
is commemorated by her splendid foundations at Oxford and
Cambridge. She was the daughter of John Beaufort, duke
of Somerset, and married, first, Edmund Tudor, earl of
Richmond, who died in 1456, by whom she had one son.
She married, secondly, Thomas Stanley, earl of Derby, whose
second wife she was. He died in 1504, and she survived
him five years, dying at length in the same year as her son,
Henry VII. Any little hereditary title Henry had to the crown
he derived from her.

Though Henry VIII. bequeathed his body to be buried
at Windsor, beside Queen Jane, his descendants and those
of his father were laid here. The monument of Edward VI.,
if indeed any special memorial to him ever existed, was
destroyed in 1643. The body rests in a shallow vault, which
Dean Stanley opened in 1868. The leaden coffin was found
to be 'rent and deformed,' as well as wasted by long corrosion,
and perhaps injured by having been examined before. Close
to it were some portions of Torregiano's altar, which were

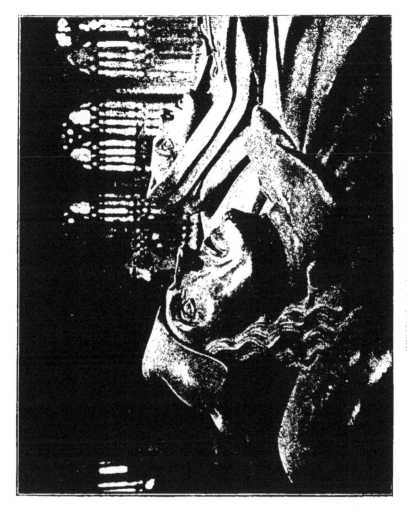

EFFIGIES OF HENRY VII. AND QUEEN.

now taken out, and worked into the present stone Communion Table.

The body of Queen Mary lies in the same grave with that of her sister. She was the first person buried in the north aisle. No monument commemorates her, other than the brief lines on Elizabeth's tomb: 'Regno consortes et urna hic obdormimus Elizabetha et Maria sorores, in spe resurrectionis.'

The universal grief of the nation at the death of Queen Elizabeth is reflected in the magnificence of the noble monument raised by James I. The artists employed would seem by their names to have been foreigners—Maximilian Powtran and John de Critz.

And now we come to a very singular fact. Queen Elizabeth died in 1603, and since that date no fewer than twelve sovereigns—or, counting Mary II., thirteen, and Oliver Cromwell, fourteen—have sat on the throne, yet no monument was ever erected to any single one of them, nor even so much as a line of inscription carved. Dean Stanley, to whom the royal sepulchres owe so much, placed these names as nearly as possible over the place where each one was buried. From this we learn that James I., Charles II., William and Mary, Queen Anne, and George II. were laid in these vaults, as well as their consorts and many of their children. The Stuart vault is at the east end of the south aisle; that of the house of Hanover in the centre of the chapel near the west door.

Another singular thing is to be noted, namely, that the last royal tomb erected in the Abbey was the monument of Mary Stuart, placed over her remains when James I. transferred them from Peterborough in 1606. In many respects it resembles that of the rival queen in the north aisle, and is no doubt by the same pair of artists. Both are,

Fan Vaulting in
South Aisle,
Henry VII Chapel

of course, wholly incongruous to the style of the building in which they are erected.

The effigies are probably portraits, but if so have a curious family likeness.

We have notices of several royal funerals by a contemporary

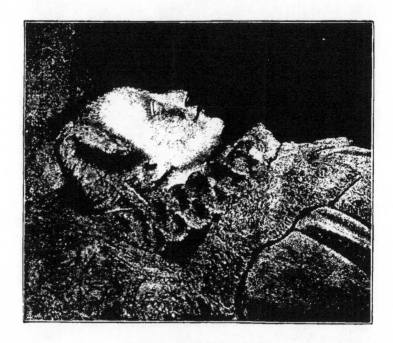

TOMB OF QUEEN MARY STUART.

writer, Henry Machyn, a citizen of London and professional herald, or perhaps undertaker, under Edward VI., Mary, and Elizabeth. In 1553 he writes particulars of the burial of Edward VI. :—

'At his burying was the greatest moan made for him of his death as ever was heard or seen, both of all sorts of people, weeping and lamenting.

And first of all went a great company of children in their surplices, and clerks singing, and then his father's bedesmen, and then two heralds, and then a standard with a dragon, and then a great number of his servants in black, and another standard with a white greyhound, and then after a great number of his officers, and after them comes more heralds, and then a standard of the head officers of his house; and then heralds: Norroy (King of Arms) bore the helmet and the crest on horseback, and then his

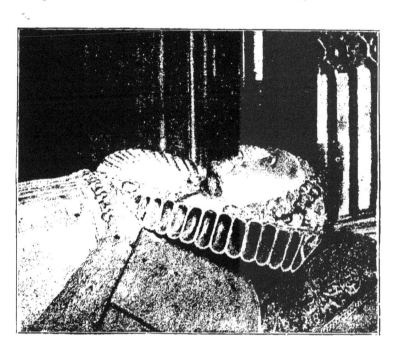

MONUMENT OF QUEEN ELIZABETH.

great banner of arms in embroidery, and with divers other banners; and then came riding Master Clarenceux (King of Arms) with his target, with his garter and his sword, gorgeously and rich, and after Garter (the principal King of Arms) with his coat armour in embroidery, and then more heralds of arms; and then came the chariot with great horses draped with velvet to the ground, and every horse having a man on his back in black, and every one bearing a banner-roll of divers kings' arms and with escutcheons on their horses, and the chariot covered with cloth of gold, and on the chariot lay a picture' (an effigy coloured like life, no doubt, is meant by *picture*) 'lying righteously with a crown of gold, and a great collar, and his sceptre in his hand, lying in his robes, and the garter about his leg, and a coat in embroidery of gold.'

He goes on at some length further, but the above must suffice. His spelling is very wonderful, and his meaning is not always clear in consequence. For example, he speaks of the effigy as 'lyeng recheussly.' Strype, in quoting the passage, changed *recheussly* into *piteously;* but I venture to think Machyn meant righteously, that is, with the hands in an attitude of prayer.

The next ceremony approaching the proportions of a royal funeral was that of Anne of Cleves. She was buried with all the ceremonial of the old church by the monks whom Queen Mary had brought back to Westminster. Her tomb, never completed, is on the south side of the altar in the Abbey, close to where the portrait of Richard II. now hangs.

As the royal interments after that of Queen Elizabeth are, as I have observed, unmarked by monuments, they hardly concern us here; but it may be well to mention that, in addition to the vault under the shrine of Henry VII., which contains the bodies of that King, his Queen, and James I., there are at least two other royal vaults, still unmentioned. The whole floor of the chapel is, in fact, honeycombed with graves. Anne of Denmark is buried on the north side of the shrine; her son, Henry, with his elder brother, a child, and Mary Stuart, his grandmother, no fewer than eighteen children of Queen Anne, and a great many other scions of royalty, are buried in the south aisle in a large vault opened by Dean Stanley. At the eastern end of the same aisle is the vault of Charles II., which contains also the bodies of

HENRY VII.'S CHAPEL. LOOKING WEST.

William III., Queen Mary, Queen Anne, and Prince George
of Denmark.   Finally, at the western end of the central aisle
is a large vault, of which plans and views have been published,
in which are buried George II., Queen Caroline, the Prince
Frederick and Princess of Wales, two Dukes of Cumberland,
and a round half-dozen of princes and princesses.   These
vaults are all immediately underneath, and a few inches only
below, the pavement.

VII

TRIFORIUM

The Seamy Side—Up-stairs in Westminster Abbey—The Angels of the Transept—The Pancake Monument—Remains in the Triforium—The Muniment-room—The Chapel of the Annunciation—The Tomb of Katharine of Valois—Pepys' Birthday Treat—The Great Reliquary— The Waxworks—Charles II.—Monk—William and Mary—Duchess of Richmond—Queen Anne—The Duke of Buckingham—The Duchess and her Son—The Organ.

IT used to be asserted by the prophets and advocates of the Gothic revival that one great characteristic of the style is the equal finish of every part of a building. Their stock apophthegm related to an ancient Greek sculptor, who, being asked why he took as much pains with the back of a statue as with the front, although it was to be hidden from view, replied, 'The gods see that.' The hidden parts of a building were carved and moulded as well as those easily visible. Unfortunately, this opinion is not borne out by facts. There is 'a seamy side' to Westminster Abbey, as well as to Canterbury Cathedral, and many another. In this chapter it may be amusing to read some notes made 'up-stairs,' in that strange region which is invisible from below, but which to an architect is perhaps the most interesting part of the church, the part in which he can best study the method of the design and the construction. Many things which are puzzling from below may be understood when we see them at closer quarters, and little changes and developments of style can be traced. We can, for example, see the difference between those arches of the nave which were made by Henry III. and Edward I. and those which were made at a much later period, when the characteristic English Perpendicular had begun to prevail. The anxiety of the later architect, perhaps Abbot Litlington (1362—1386), to imitate exactly the work done under Ware (1258—1284) a century earlier, is clearly shown. Thus, at the north-eastern angle of the nave there is a window of which the eastern jamb is of the work of Henry III. and the western of that of Edward I. So, too, when we have traced Edward's work for five bays westward, we come upon a window in which one jamb is of the time of Richard II. In the triforium all these junctions are very clearly marked, sometimes even by a change of level; but the greatest change of all is in the greater purity, delicacy, and freedom of the oldest work.

The triforium is the place from which we can best see those famous sculptures known as 'the censing angels.' The artist who placed these figures in the north and south transepts must have had a genius which brought him nearer to the great Greek sculptors of the Periclean period than any who has lived since their time. What must the central statues have been like to be worthy of such accessories? Sir G. Scott hardly appreciates their beauty; they represent, he says, 'angels censing, and are exceedingly fine, after making due allowance for the height at which they were intended to have been seen.' But they look even better when seen as close as we can get in the triforium; and perhaps if one had to select the best public statue in England, it would be impossible to overlook the claims of

the angel in the north transept on the western side. He
appears to be literally hovering in the air, or, rather—for
this the sculptor has most marvellously expressed—he is
supposed to be swinging his censer in the presence of his
Lord, and to be floating in a sea of light, which forces him
to bow his head and avert his face from its dazzling effulgence.
Many other beautiful carvings may be inspected at close
quarters from the triforium, and, I am sorry to say, some
that have been removed from the church. Among these
is a monument which might be selected as at the opposite
end of the scale in sculpture from the angels of the transepts.
This is the famous 'pancake monument'—a memorial of
Admiral Tyrrell, put up in 1766, or thereabouts. Perhaps
the figure of Sir Cloudesley Shovel, in Roman armour and
a full wig, is quite as bad; but it is neither so large nor so
obtrusive as the 'pancake monument' was. Now it no longer
blocks up a window, and some people may be pleased at
its removal. I do not share this view. There are plenty of
other windows quite as fine as this one; there was only one
such example of the taste of the middle of the last century.
It certainly was very ugly, but it was also very curious;
and other windows, as, for instance, those to Locke and
Stephenson, are practically blocked up, but with glass, not
marble, and are ugly without being in the least curious.
The pancakes, and the sea, and cherubs' heads, are all in
the triforium, and among them the figure of the Admiral, all
nude, and white, and ghastly—a sad example of the mutability
of fame. It was sculptured, and we may presume designed,
by Nicholas Read, an unworthy pupil of Roubiliac. I
mention the probability that he designed it, because there is
another work of his in the Abbey, which was only executed
by him from the design of Robert Adam. This is the fine

monument to the Duchess of Northumberland in the Chapel
of St. Nicholas, and is open to no objection on the score
of taste.

Before we leave the triforium we must glance at the rows
of undertakers' helmets, some with, some without, the crests;
at the fragments already mentioned of the reredos of the
Chapel of Henry VII.; at a small portion of Inigo Jones's
reredos from the choir; at a vast cope chest, the only one
remaining; and we must not neglect to look down into
the Muniment-room. This curious apartment is over that
portion of the cloister which occupies the place of the western
aisle of the south transept. When Henry III. rebuilt the
church, the old cloister of Edward the Confessor was left
standing, and here, where it interfered with the new design,
the church was built over it. The space between the roof
of the cloister and the floor of the triforium in this part,
then, is utilised as a Muniment-room, and is filled with
coffers, some of them dating back, probably, to the thirteenth
century.

Merely glancing at the curious little obelisks in wood carved
and gilt, which once stood at the entrance of the choir, we may
descend the dark and narrow staircase which takes us down
into the eastern walk of the cloister, very glad to find ourselves
on the ground again. Except to a well-practised head, the
giddy height is extremely disagreeable. There are no railings
to protect the visitor who wishes to peer down into the church,
where men and women walking about look like crawling ants.
There are narrow passes, too, where a stout person can
scarcely squeeze through, and everywhere it is necessary to
walk very circumspectly, for in some places the floor is very
irregular, in others there is very little light, and there are
treacherous pipes, blocks of stone covered with old carving,

The Choir
Herbert Railton

G

and other obstructions ready to trip you up. Unquestionably, however, the one view from the extreme east end towards the west door, and the diagonal view across the choir and into the south transept, or Poets' Corner, are worth a good deal of trouble and personal risk.

The chantry of Henry V. is one of the strangest places in the Abbey. It cannot, of course, be made available for the general sight-seer, being approached only by narrow newel staircases, which open just at the feet of Queen Philippa and Queen Eleanor on either side, and being moreover of very delicate, not to say rickety, construction. The view of 'long-drawn aisle and fretted vault' looking westward is very fine. Under the stone altar-slab lie the remains of Katharine, the widow of the King; secretly the wife, at the time of her death, of Owen Tudor, the keeper of her wardrobe, by whom she became the ancestress of the Tudor dynasty. Dean Stanley, in a curious account of a visit of Henry VI. to the Abbey to choose a place for his own burial, makes the mistake of thinking that in 1460 the coffin of the Queen, who had died in January 1438, was still unburied. The document from which he quotes, however, makes it plain that not only was she buried, but that a tomb of some kind had been placed over her remains. It was proposed to remove it, to 'apparel' it better, and to leave room for the King's grave before the altar of the Lady Chapel. This was never done; and the Queen's remains rested in the centre of the chapel, near the feet of her first husband. The exact spot must have been where the steps begin to ascend into the great Lady Chapel of Henry VII. When his wonderful building was projected the coffin was taken up, but Henry declared his intention of burying it suitably in his new chapel. This, for some reason, was never done; and the remains of the Queen, dried up like a mummy,

Two Bays of Triforium

were seen and touched by many visitors to the Abbey. Pepys
records that, in 1669, 'here we did see, by particular favour,
the body of Queen Katharine of Valois; and I had the upper
part of her body in my hands, and I did kiss her mouth;
reflecting upon it that I did kiss a queen, and that this was my
birthday, thirty-six years old, that I did kiss a queen.' After
mentioning this ghastly birthday treat, Pepys goes on to correct
the prevalent impression that she had never been buried.
Hearne, the antiquary, in the next century, called some
attention to the indecent exhibition; bringing down on himself
the wrath of the Abbey vergers, who made money by it. In
1776 the coffin was placed in concealment under the Villiers
monument in the Chapel of St. Nicholas, and Dean Stanley
had it brought up to its present resting-place one hundred and
two years later. The altar dedicated to the Annunciation is
plain and massive. On the front is an inscription in Latin,
stating that it contains the bones of Queen Katharine, but I am
credibly informed that a very small proportion of the skeleton
was rescued from the spoliation of relic-worshippers and
thieves. Behind the altar and at either side we can see the
marks of the cupboards in which before the Reformation the
relics of saints and other treasures of the Church were preserved. The great reliquary had stood below, very near where
the tomb of Henry V. was afterwards placed, and, no doubt,
this chantry, from its comparative inaccessibility, was found
very convenient for the purpose. The wooden shutters of the
presses have been removed, but the marks of the hinges may
still be seen, and there are places which seem to have been
designed for candlesticks. Standing at the low wall on the
westward side, we can look down into the Confessor's Chapel,
and keen sight can detect within the upper structure of the
tomb, that part which is sometimes attributed to Abbot

Feckenham, sometimes to James II., a coffin apparently
clamped with iron, which is supposed to contain the body of
the royal saint.

The waxworks of Westminster Abbey have not been seen
by many people, but are deservedly famous. At first, as mentioned in a former chapter, it was customary when a king or
any other great personage was to be buried to place on the
coffin his effigy formed of boiled leather. When the art of
modelling in '*cuir bouilli*' was lost, wax was employed for
making the image, and wax, notwithstanding its proverbial
pliancy, is a very enduring substance. From the north aisle of
the apse we ascend a narrow staircase, passing by the way some
of the most beautiful sculpture in the Abbey, fronting the
chapel of Abbot Islip. At a turn in the stair which leads to
a kind of upper gallery we are suddenly confronted with the
lifelike figure of King Charles II., whose face, as rendered
familiar by numerous and contemporary engravings, with its
black eyes and swarthy complexion, looks out from behind the
glass of a cupboard only a few inches from the spot we have
reached. The royal figure is dressed in crimson velvet, now
sadly browned, and adorned with the finest lace of the period.

When we have recovered composure and breath, and can
look round, we find ourselves in the presence of a series of
most interesting and curious portraits. The wooden presses,
with glass fronts, are, to judge from the pattern of the hinges,
of about the time of the monarch whose effigy was the first to
confront us. The rest, taken chronologically, consist of ten
figures beginning with Queen Elizabeth and ending with Lord
Nelson, but neither of these, the first and last, were really
funeral effigies. Queen Elizabeth's was made in 1760, as part
of the commemoration of the bicentenary of the Collegiate
Church. The original figure was worn out by exhibition before

1708, when it is described as in the last stage of dilapidation,
so that the oldest figure we see is that of General Monk, who
is more correctly described as the Duke of Albemarle. A
headless 'torso' of James I. is on the top of one cupboard, and
a number of fragments are in a closed case, probably those of
the series mentioned by Stow, which began with Edward III.
The Duke of Albemarle's figure is in poor condition, having
sunk in stature to a height of about four feet. It is in the
armour of the time—a steel breastplate and jack-boots—but
the famous cap, celebrated by Goldsmith and Barham, in
which, after taking visitors round, the vergers used to collect
their fees, has long disappeared. Monk died in January, 1670,
and the preparations for his public funeral were not complete
before the end of April. His body was laid in a vault near the
head of the monument of Queen Elizabeth, and his wife, who
died between the time of his death and his funeral, beside him.
In the same vault, and not, as is often supposed, in the marble
urn in which the bones were removed from the Tower, are
buried the remains supposed to be those of Edward V. and his
brother, which were discovered in 1674. Monk's monument is
in the other aisle of this same chapel of Henry VII., and there
stood the effigy for a century or more after the funeral. It
was in fact his only monument for fifty years, till, after the
death of his son, a monument without any inscription was put
up by Scheemakers from a design by Kent.

The figure of Charles II. comes next in order, and is followed
by that of his niece, Queen Mary, whose effigy is accompanied
in the same case with that of her husband, William III. She
died of small-pox in 1695, and this may give her face the
drawn, pinched look it wears, for it is modelled from a
plaster cast taken after death. William, who survived her
till 1702, is also evidently modelled from the original, even

to the figure which shows his short stature. He stands upon a pillow to raise his head to a level with that of the Queen.

Next in chronological order comes the figure of Frances Theresa, widow of the last Duke of Richmond and Lennox. She is known in history as 'la belle Stewart,' and is said to have sat for the figure of Britannia on our coinage. She was the daughter of Walter Stewart, a scion of the Blantyre family. The Duchess died on the 15th of October, 1702, the very year of Queen Anne's coronation, and is represented in the robes she wore at that ceremonial, having left orders that she was to be 'as well done in wax as can be.' Beside her, on a perch, is a favourite grey parrot, which, having lived with her forty years, died a few days after her.

Next we come to Queen Anne. Her effigy does not by any means confirm the usual ideas about either her mind or her appearance. Her expression as we see it in this image is extremely pleasing, but, more than that, it is the expression of an extremely capable, and, indeed, clever woman, of great force of character. If it is a portrait, as we have every reason to believe, it greatly enhances our ideas of her personal charms, representing her probably more as she had been about the age of thirty than as a gouty woman of fifty. She wears a robe of silk brocade, and her hair flows over her shoulders. Queen Anne died on the 1st of August, 1714.

A family group follows. The Duchess of Buckingham had three sons, of whom one lived but three weeks, and the second, who was born in 1711, and also died young, is represented as standing by her. He died in 1715, at the age of three years and seven weeks, but appears older in his effigy. Opposite the glass case which contains this child and his mother is the ghastly figure of her third son, Edmund, who succeeded to his father's titles, and died at Rome at the early age of eighteen, in 1735. The effigy shows the young Duke as a corpse, arrayed in the robes of a peer, with a coronet. It is curious to remark that this is the only waxwork in which the deceased is represented as a recumbent figure. The funeral took place on the 31st of January, 1736, and was the last in which an effigy was laid on the coffin. The figures of Chatham and Nelson were merely made for exhibition, though it is said that a real uniform of Nelson's is on his effigy.

We have one more climb to make, but comparatively a short one. It is not known for certain whether there was an organ in the church before the Reformation, but it is exceedingly probable. After the Restoration 'Father Smith' placed a small instrument over two arches on the north side over the stalls. Immediately underneath are the graves of the old organists— Blow, Purcell, and Croft. The organ as it is now, though not the largest built in this country, is probably the most complete in modern appliances and scientific action. It was finished in 1884, and replaced the instrument built by Schrieder and Jordan in 1730. Many additions were made to the old organ during the following century, but there were certain radical defects according to modern ideas which could not be remedied. In the 'Engineer' of August 12th, 1885, will be found a full scientific account of this new organ, from which we take the following details :—'The action of the instrument, with the sole exception of the choir manual touch, is entirely on the tubular pneumatic system. The same general principle is applied in the case of the great, swell, solo, and pedal touches, which are all perfectly light and easy to play on, whether couplers are used or not.' The total length of the metal tubing is considerably over two miles. Above the pedals are ten combination pedals, which act upon the great, swell, and pedal stops. The bellows are in the cloister vault, at a distance of sixty feet. The solo stops are forty-five feet from the pavement, so that they have great acoustical advantages. The first musical performance given on the new organ consisted almost entirely of the composition of the Abbey organists, from Henry Purcell's anthem, 'Oh, sing unto the Lord,' to the 'Magnificat' in G of Dr. J. F. Bridge.

VIII

THE POETS' CORNER AND THE
CHAPTER-HOUSE

Literature in Westminster Abbey—Ingulph of Croyland—Matthew of
Westminster—The Scriptorium—Geoffrey Chaucer—William Caxton
—The Duchess of Burgundy—The Red Pale—Easteney and Islip
—Maud Caxton—Poetry and Poverty—Spenser, Jonson, Butler,
Dryden—Cenotaphs—The Busts—Dickens—Lytton—Dean Stanley's
Funeral—The Library—The Chapter House—A Roman Sarcophagus.

THE first literary man in the strict sense of the word
whom we find at Westminster was Ingulph, afterwards
a monk at Croyland, whose 'Chronicle' has of late years been
received as genuine, though it certainly used to be looked
upon with suspicion. Ingulph relates some reminiscences of
his school days at Westminster. It was in the reign of
Edward the Confessor, and the Normans had not yet come
over the sea. Frequently, he says, he saw the Lady Edith.
His father was employed about the Court, and he was at
school in the Abbey, and the lady used to meet him as he
came home and question him as to his studies. He specially
remarked upon her acuteness in reasoning; 'she would catch
me,' he adds, 'with the subtle threads of her arguments.'
But she did not forget to 'tip' the school-boy, nor yet to
gratify another instinct which his modern representative also
shares. When three or four pieces of money had been

counted out to him by her handmaiden he was sent to the

Chaucers Tomb.

larder to refresh himself. No wonder Ingulph had in after

years a lively and grateful recollection of his school days at
Westminster.

There seems to have been a writing-school, or *scriptorium*,
in the cloisters. Till lately the grooves made in the stonework
to fit the desks to it could be plainly traced in the north walk.
Such marks were of course very obnoxious to the eyes of a
'restorer,' as helping to elucidate the history of the place,
and Sir Gilbert Scott had them carefully obliterated. What
books were written here and what kind of illumination was
practised we cannot tell for certain, but there is still in the
Library a Missal prepared in 1373 for Abbot Litlington, which,
if we could be sure it was written in the Abbey Scriptorium,
would go far to settle the question.

Geoffrey Chaucer undoubtedly lived in Westminster, and
was Clerk of the Works, or something of the kind, during
the latter part of the reign of Richard II. The authors of
the 'Deanery Guide' are of opinion that he had fallen into
poverty before his death, and that his burial in what is now
the Poets' Corner was owing to the post he held and the
position of his house in the monastery garden. It bore the
poetical sign of 'The Rose,' and was among the houses
pulled down to make way for the chapel of Henry VII.
Chaucer's monument only dates from the reign of Queen
Mary, when, amid the many destructions which had been
wrought all around, it is refreshing to find that a brother poet,
Nicholas Brigham, presented the grey marble tomb into which
the honoured bones were removed in 1555. It is probable
that Brigham was himself buried close by, and Camden
mentions the grave of a little daughter, Rachel Brigham, aged
four, as having been '*Juxta Galfridum Chaucerum*.' The
painting on the tomb and the shields of arms have long
disappeared, but the great galaxy of writers who shone during

the reign of Elizabeth were not likely to forget 'Dan Chaucer,' and his grave consecrated the south transept as the cemetery of English poets. Chaucer was buried in 1400, and reburied in 1555, and in 1599 the body of Edmund Spenser was interred close by, so that, as a contemporary poet said in some Latin verses quoted by Camden, he that was nearest to Chaucer in genius should have his grave next to him.

During the hundred and ninety-nine years which divided the death of Chaucer from that of Spenser the greatest event in the history of English literature had taken place in West-minster, namely, the introduction of the art of printing.

Caxton had been engaged in commerce at Bruges, and had risen to be the head of the English Merchant Adventurers. As a Merchant Adventurer he could not marry, and, no doubt, it was for love of the Maud Caxton who was buried in St. Margaret's in 1490, twenty-nine years later, that he relinquished trade, went into the household of the Duchess, and, to amuse her, translated into English a French compila-tion named 'Le Recueil des Histoire de Troye.' The Duchess was a sister of our Edward IV. Mr. Blades tells us all about Caxton's subsequent translations and compilations, and how, at length, overcome by a literary ambition, which must eventually have been abundantly satisfied, he left Bruges, where Colard Mansion had taught him how to multiply copies of his romances, and coming to Westminster settled down there for the brief but busy remainder of his life. His activity was prodigious. He was, we must remember, author, compositor, printer, binder, and publisher, all in one. The house he took for his work was in the Almonry, that is, adjoining on the south side to the western gate, but within the precincts. The sign it bore was the Red Pale ; but whether the heraldic term is here meant, or there was a red pale set up over the door, we cannot tell now. Near it, says Stow, writing about a century later, was an old chapel of St. Anne, and an almshouse founded by the mother of Henry VII. Stow makes mention of the establishment of the first English printing-press, which he attributes to the patronage of Abbot Islip. This patronage Mr. Blades will not allow, partly on the ground that when Caxton came over in 1476 Easteney, and not Islip, was Abbot. But probably Islip, as a prominent official of the Abbey, was more concerned than his superior in selecting a printing-house and settling Caxton in it; and when Caxton says the lord abbot 'did do show' him certain evidences, by what hands could this have been accomplished better than by those of Islip, who was then a rising and active subordinate, and had filled successively all the offices below that of prior, to which he was elected shortly before he became Abbot? True, he did not become Abbot till after Caxton's death; but Stow must not be convicted of inaccuracy because he gives him the title he bore for more than thirty years.

During the fifteen years Caxton continued to print at the Red Pale—the site of which, by the way, is not inaptly marked by the red granite pillar in front of the entrance to Dean's Yard—he issued, besides works which are lost or unidentified, no fewer than ninety-nine different publications, some of them, like the 'Canterbury Tales' of Chaucer, books of considerable size. Caxton had a particular veneration for Chaucer, and put up a brass 'epitaphy' over his grave, the only memorial till 1555. Of the poet he says in an epilogue, 'in all his works he excelleth in my opinion on all other writers in our English, for he writeth no void words, but all his matter is full of high and quick sentence, to whom ought to be given laud and praising for his noble making and writing.'

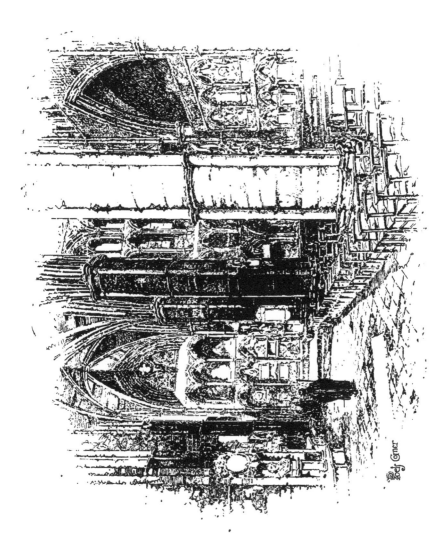

It is very sad in looking down the lists of poets buried in the Poets' Corner in any guide-book, like that compiled by the Miss Bradleys for example, to see repeated, over and over again, the same melancholy formula, 'died in poverty.' The first of the poets laid here, Chaucer, 'fell into poverty in his old age.' Spenser, according to Drummond of Hawthornden, 'died for lake of bread' in King's Street, Westminster. Yet he had something very like a public funeral, all the literary men of the day assembling round his grave, and casting into it odes in his memory, and the pens with which they were written. Ben Jonson 'died in great poverty' in a house on the north side of the Abbey, near St. Margaret's Church. He was buried in the nave in an upright position, having been promised ground two feet by two in his lifetime either by the King or by the Dean. His remains have been seen several times since, when other graves have been dug close by. The simple epitaph, 'O Rare Ben Jonson,' was cut, it is said, at the cost of Sir John Young, 'who, walking here when the grave was covering, gave the fellow eighteen-pence to cut it.' Another poet commemorated here, Butler, the writer of 'Hudibras,' also died 'in great poverty,' as is recorded in the well-known epigram :—

> 'When Butler, needy wretch ! was yet alive,
> No generous patron would a dinner give.
> Behold him, starved to death and turned to dust,
> Presented with a monumental bust.
> The poet's fate is here in emblem shown :
> He asked for bread, and he received a stone.'

The great 'Ann Dorset Pembroke and Montgomery' set up the monuments of Drayton and Spenser; and John Sheffield, duke of Buckingham, of whom we shall see more

THE CHAPTER-HOUSE.

H

in another chapter, that of Dryden, who also, we read, 'died in great poverty.' Many of the other monuments in this transept have similarly been dedicated by admiring friends and patrons. That of Milton, for example, has been satirised as having on it more about Benson, who set it up, than about the poet. David Garrick was buried among the poets in 1779, and his monument, 'the tribute of a friend, was erected in 1797.' The Duke and Duchess of Queensberry made Gay's tomb and put on it above Pope's epitaph the brief couplet he wrote for himself:—

> 'Life is a jest, and all things show it:
> I thought so once, but now I know it.'

I confess to a feeling of weariness at the number of 'cenotaphs' we see here. A cenotaph is defined as the monument of a person buried elsewhere; and the Poets' Corner is crammed with such memorials, and especially with busts. Anstey, Sharp, Goldsmith, Coleridge, Thomson, Thackeray, and many others, are buried elsewhere, and of some of them no memorial is needed here. This is especially true of Shakespeare and Milton. The one sleeps in the church of St. Giles, Cripplegate, the other in his own Stratford-on-Avon. An opposite case is that of Dr. Johnson, who, though he is buried here, has a monument in St. Paul's. The busts, set simply on brackets, and not forming part of any architectural composition, are also disagreeable to the eye in proportion as from their prominence they intrude themselves upon the sight. Keble's absurd nude bust is not, as it should be, in the Poets' Corner, but in the baptistery, which has indeed been sometimes called the Deputy Poets' Corner; but in reality all the monuments of poets here, Keble's, Herbert's, Cowper's, Wordsworth's, and Kingsley's, are cenotaphs. There is only a gravestone over Charles Dickens, in the south transept; and, in truth, it is a pity his body was not buried, as it is understood he wished himself, in Rochester Cathedral. Here, among so many greater men, he is lost. Another, and very typical example of the professional literary men of the generation just gone by, was Lord Lytton, whose grave is very near, but not in the Poets' Corner. He rests among princes and princesses in the Chapel of St. Edmund.

I am making no attempt to enumerate the literary monuments of Westminster Abbey, but there is one in the Chapel of Henry VII. which can scarcely be overlooked. Dean Stanley wrote very little in verse, but his prose is more poetical than much contemporary 'poetry,' and has a singular sweetness and a charm which cannot be defined. The recumbent statue, which has since been placed over the grave, is by the late Sir J. Boehm, R.A., and is very beautiful and appropriate, and, what is of more importance perhaps, a marvellously faithful likeness.

The Library closely adjoins both the Poets' Corner and also the Chapter-house. The passage from the south transept, which formerly led to the monks' dormitory from the church, passes across the entrance to the Chapter-house, ending in the Library, which forms the northern part of the building containing the great school-room. There is here a considerable collection of old books, many on divinity, and a few very beautiful manuscripts. The room itself is worth seeing, but is not generally shown to the public. The library was founded, or refounded, by John Williams, the last Churchman who held the Great Seal of England, and both Dean of Westminster and Archbishop of York, a great opponent of Laud. He bought a large private library, and

placed it in what was then 'a waste room,' which he furnished
and adorned for it. The collection is remarkable for the
bindings of many of the books, which are very ancient and
curious, and well worthy of inspection in these days when
so many people make binding a fine art. Among the
manuscripts is one on natural history, with pictures which
remind us of the animals depicted on the western wall of
the Chapter-house below. It would be interesting to compare
these two productions of mediaeval art and science.

The Chapter-house is, perhaps, in its design and proportions
one of the most beautiful features of the Abbey. Yet,
until our own day, it was miserably neglected, and in great
danger of a complete downfall. The most determined
opponent of 'restoration' must approve the greater part of
the work carried out here by Sir Gilbert Scott, in 1865 and
subsequent years. The place had been used by the House
of Commons up to the time of Edward VI., who allowed the
members to sit in St. Stephen's Chapel. At the dissolution
of the Abbey the Chapter-house became Crown property, and,
I believe, continues to belong to the State. The chamber
called 'Jerusalem' has long been the real Chapter-house.
The State records were stowed in various places, such as the
Tower and parts of the old Palace of Westminster; and very
soon after the dissolution the Chapter-house was fitted up
for a similar purpose. The result has been a benefit to us;
because, instead of the destruction and defacement which
went on elsewhere, here everything was covered with the
cupboards and boxes containing the rapidly accumulating
collection of State papers. The worst misfortune the building
underwent also proved a blessing in disguise. The upper
part of the vault was taken down as dangerous in 1740, and a
flat ceiling substituted. Had this not been done we should

have lost the whole building, owing to the insufficiently supported thrust of the vaulting, and the failure in places of the foundations.   Scott, who was as much an engineer as an architect, counteracted the thrust by iron-work concealed in the vaulting, and by restoring the buttresses which look so large outside.

As the Chapter-house stands now, it is a singularly noble building.   Approached from a low and rather dark passage, and by a flight of steps, the whole effect of the interior bursts on the visitor suddenly.   It is often compared with the Chapter-house at Salisbury, and there are many points of resemblance between them, but this is the earlier of the two.   The height to the crown of the vaulting is about fifty-four feet, the central pillar being about thirty-five feet in height.   The wooden flooring concealed and preserved for us a very nearly complete example of an encaustic tile pavement.   The paintings on the eastern wall should be carefully examined while they are yet visible. Unfortunately, by way of securing their preservation, they were coated by some sort of varnish by Scott, and the past few years have wrought more harm to them than the centuries they passed in neglect behind the wainscoting of the Record Office.   The chamber is still in a sense a record office, and the visitor will see in the glass cases many curiosities of literature, among them some fragments of paper found in a rat's hole, on which are a few lines of Caxton's printing. There is also a fine show of the oldest of the Abbey charters, several of which have been already described in our earlier chapters.   Lastly, before leaving the place, we should take a look at the stone coffin near the entrance.   It has been a puzzle to antiquaries, having been found in the green space north of the nave, and having on its side a Latin inscription

in the old Roman style; and what looks like a twelfth-century
Christian cross on the lid.   It is most probably an ancient
Roman sarcophagus appropriated by some mediaeval monk
for his own interment, and completed by the addition of
the crossed lid.   There are some Norman carvings preserved
also in this vestibule, which will help us to an idea of the
style and decoration of the church commenced by Edward
the Confessor.

IX

THE HERALDRY

Very Ancient Shields—Simon Montfort, Earl of Leicester—William Valence, Earl of Pembroke—Aveline Forts—Aylmer Valence—Queen Eleanor—Edward III.—Richard II.—Henry V.—The Chapel of St. Edmund—A Decaying Art—Humphrey Bourchier—The Countess of Stafford—The Duchess of Suffolk—Grants of Arms—Quarterings—Sir Lewis Robsert—Chapel of Henry VII.—Heraldry of the Poets' Corner —Of the Nave.

THE Abbey is a museum of heraldic devices. True, it has not the Garter plates of St. George's Chapel at Windsor, but, on the other hand, it has a few relics of the shields put up by Henry III., which rank among the most ancient examples of the kind now remaining. The fashion of using coats-of-arms had been slowly growing, but of heraldry, in the strict sense of the word, there was none until the end of the reign of King John at the earliest. A great deal has been written to the contrary, especially by the professional heralds, and a great deal of dust has been thrown in the eyes of inquiring antiquaries; but the doubtful and obscure shields to be seen on seals are almost all that can be found of an earlier date than the fine series in the Abbey, of which unhappily so little remains. There cannot be much doubt that heraldry originated in the East, and was brought home by the Crusaders. The Sultans of Egypt, in the ninth century and later, had shields of arms. It has sometimes, rather conjecturally, been asserted that each coat of this ancient series in the Abbey represents a benefactor of the church, or some one who contributed to the building fund. Fourteen only remain, but there are several more of a very slightly later date, not so large, and painted only, not carved. They are attached to little heads of men or birds by loops, and these heads may possibly offer us the first idea of supporters; but as yet neither crests nor supporters have come into use. The heraldic proportions so much insisted upon had not been clearly laid down, and the 'bordure bezantee' of the arms of the Earl of Cornwall is so narrow that there is hardly room for the coins. The birds in the arms assigned to Edward the Confessor have their feet. Later heraldry prescribed that a 'martlet' had no feet. The eagle displayed, representing the empire, has only one head, and the arms of St. Louis are 'semee' of fleurs-de-lis. It is easily seen that these are the early experiments in the science, and were made before the fixing of hard-and-fast rules for the guidance of the artist.

One realises the history of the time better after looking at the shield of Simon, the stout Earl of Leicester, who is always credited with the invention of parliamentary government. He must have stood just here and looked at this very shield when it was first put up, years before his final quarrel with Henry and the fatal field of Evesham.

Very soon heraldry was corrupted. Hard-and-fast rules were made. Coats became strictly hereditary, and the bearings lost the freedom and simplicity they had at first. Of the same period as the fourteen shields described above, but of foreign, not English workmanship, is the coat-of-arms on the monument of William Valence, earl of Pembroke, King Henry's half-brother, in the Chapel of St. Edmund. He died at Bayonne in 1296. The tomb is richly ornamented with Limoges enamel, the armour and the arms being most highly elaborated, and the pillow covered with a kind of diaper, formed of the arms of England and of Valence. His shield hangs on his left side, and by the arrangement of a mirror it is possible to examine it very closely. The work is of the kind known as *champlevé*. Mr. William Burges was both a good herald and also a good judge of enamel, and he pronounced the whole monument to have been made at Limoges, and sent over here.

Among the older shields is that of the Earl of Albemarle. His name is always given in the Latin form, 'de Fortibus,' and was probably in English 'Forts' or 'Fortes.' He had an only daughter, Aveline, the greatest heiress of her time, and Henry III. married her to his second son, Edmund. She did not long survive her marriage, and lies buried on the north side of the sacrarium, under a stone tomb, which has been the admiration of every generation for its simple, severe dignity, and exquisite proportion. She was married in 1270, being then in her eighteenth year, and the sculptor represents her at about that age. She is sometimes said to have died in the year of her marriage, and cannot, in any case, have lived much longer, for her husband married again in 1274. Although the sculpture is of the most delicate and finished character, the artist was not content with the effect produced until he had ornamented every part with painting and gilding. Naturally the then novel fashion of wearing heraldic devices is largely resorted to, and on her dress are still faint traces of the arms of her father as seen in the old sculptures already described. Twelve little shields at each side give his arms, those of her

mother, who was also a great heiress, with those of her
husband, and a great many besides. Other examples of old
heraldry are offered by the shields on the adjoining monuments of Aylmer Valence, son and successor of the earl
commemorated by the enamelled tomb, and of Edmund, called
Crouchback, earl of Lancaster, the husband of the Lady
Aveline. The heraldry of Earl Edmund's tomb is especially
rich, but painted only and not sculptured. To find sculptured
shields of this, the early, period of heraldry, we must go to
the monument of Queen Eleanor, where the three shields of
England, Castile (quartering Leon), and Ponthieu are repeated
on either side, but are much defaced and broken away. It is
curious to observe that there is not a single coat-of-arms on the
monuments of either Henry III. or Edward I.

The Chapel of St. Edmund is so full of the heraldry of the
real heraldic times of the thirteenth and fourteenth centuries,
as well as of the later heraldry of the Heralds' College, that it
is difficult for any one who is interested in the subject to leave
it. When the Wars of the Roses were all but over, Richard
III. founded the College, and thenceforth heraldry became
what it is still, and what Mr. Burges described it as being—an
art in a state of decay. In St. Edmund's Chapel we may
observe it in all the stages of its history. Besides the arms
which have been noticed, those of William Valence, of John of
Eltham, and of the Duchess of Gloucester, there is much else
of the kind which should be examined. Close to the tomb of
the duchess is that of Humphrey Bourchier, slain at the battle
of Barnet in 1470. The figure has disappeared, but the helmet
and curious crest remain, as well as a series of badges showing
the ' Bourchier Knot,' and a coat of quarterings. He was son
of Lord Berners, great-grandson of the Duchess of Gloucester,

whose grave is beside his, and father of the learned Lord
Berners, who made a delightful translation of the 'Chronicle'
of John Froissart. Bourchier was, undoubtedly, entitled to
quarter the old royal arms. But in the jealous days of Edward
IV. such a right was tacitly ignored. No such caution was
necessary in the case of Archbishop Richard Waldeby, of York,
who had been a friend of the Black Prince, and tutor of
Richard II. The King's arms form the chief ornament of the
canopy of his brass. That heraldry had not become fixed is
evident from this shield, on which the arms attributed to
Edward the Confessor are impaled on the dexter side with
those of Richard II. on the sinister. Many descendants of the
Duchess of Gloucester, besides Bourchier, are buried in this
chapel, among them Mary, countess of Stafford, whose husband
was one of the victims of the Popish plot agitation in the reign
of Charles II. Her Latin epitaph mentions her royal descent.
The monument of her grandson, the last earl of the family, is
one of the most singular, heraldically speaking, in the Abbey.
It consists simply of a tablet, with an epitaph and a decorative
border. The most conspicuous memorial in this chapel is,
perhaps, that of the Duchess of Suffolk, the mother of Lady
Jane Grey, and its ornamentation is almost solely heraldic.
Her epitaph says she was 'daughter to Charles Brandon, Duke
of Southfolke, and Marie, the French Qvene.' The number of
near relations this unfortunate lady lost by the hands of the
public executioner is simply frightful. Her husband, her
daughter, her son-in-law, and her son-in-law's father were
all beheaded; and during the reign of Queen Mary she
lived in retirement, and married a plain esquire named
Adrian Stock. He put up this handsome monument to her
memory, having obtained from Queen Elizabeth, with whom

she was in high favour, a special grant of arms for its better adornment.

The gorgeous, but excessive, heraldry of the seventeenth century is well illustrated also in this chapel, especially in examples of the multiplication of quarterings. The head of the Talbots of Shrewsbury, a man of the most noble descent, vies with the comparatively *parvenu* Lord Russell in this respect, and both show the orthodox sixteen quarters, the earl counting among his the arms so conspicuous on the tomb of William Valence. The tomb of Katharine Knollys is of this fashion also, but a little older than that of Shrewsbury. She also has her sixteen quarterings, and no fewer than four crests. Lady Knollys was niece of Queen Anne Boleyn, and attended her on the scaffold. Her name is given on her monument as 'the Right Honourable Lady Katharine Knollys,' on what grounds, unless by special grant of her first cousin, Queen Elizabeth, it would not be easy to say. A very good example is in the next chapel, that of St. Nicholas. It contains the arms of Elizabeth, Lady Ros, daughter of the Earl of Rutland, and wife of Sir William Cecil, a grandson of the great Lord Burleigh. The Burleigh family had already contrived to amass a shield of sixteen quarters, but they are not to be compared for nobility with those of Lady Ros, who was born a Manners, and so was descended from a sister of Edward IV. The beautiful shield of what is now the ducal house of Rutland, with its lions and fleurs-de-lis, is almost lost in the multiplicity of other arms.

The banner of Sir Lewis Robsert and a double row of small shields commemorate the King's standard-bearer at Agincourt, and offer a good sample of the heraldry of the fifteenth century. It is in the Chapel of St. Paul, and close to the tomb of the King who had led Robsert into battle. At each corner

Henry VII Chapel

is an armorial flag held up by a lion and a falcon ; and we see
much of that freedom of treatment characteristic, as we have
ventured to say, of the older heraldry.

The Chapel of Henry VII. is rich in heraldry. The banners
of the Knights of the Bath and their stall plates supply a
warmth of colour which is welcome ; and wherever we look we
see lions and roses and fleurs-de-lis, but the true mediaeval
touch has departed. The emblems are all in a stiff, formal
style, and even the royal arms on the grating round the tomb
have lost all the old freedom of treatment. There is a good
display of heraldry on the tomb in the south aisle of Lady
Lennox, and also a few simple shields on the tomb of Queen
Mary of Scotland. But the greatest display is on the monument of Queen Elizabeth, her ancestors on both sides being
commemorated, and especially her descent from the House of
York. The banners and stall plates are not worth much
trouble, but many of them date from the reign of the Georges,
and some interesting names may be found.

Very few of the monuments in the nave were without
heraldry till the last century ; but there are not many worth
pausing at. While the science was yet alive great folks were
buried in the chapels, and there are only a few simple shields
of the modern book-plate type to be seen. The statesmen in
the north transept seem to have patronised heraldry as little as
the poets in the south transept. But the well-known arms of
Chaucer are sculptured on his monument, and a few others
occur, as, for example, those of Drayton, who has 'a pegasus
volant.' Gay also has his arms, and so has Rowe, the translator
of Lucan's ' Pharsalia.'

There is nothing in Westminster Abbey like the long series
of shields which ornament the cloisters of Canterbury Cathedral,

nor are many of the bosses of the roof adorned with heraldry.
It has been almost wholly neglected in the modern monuments.
An exception must be made for that of Dean Stanley, whose
arms, with those of his wife, Lady Augusta Bruce, and many
well-executed badges, are in a window beside the tomb.   The
arms of Mr. George Edmund Street, R.A., and of Sir Gilbert
Scott, the architects, are on their brasses in the nave, and show,
by the way, a curious similarity, both consisting of a not very
common device, three St. Catherine's wheels.

X

THE MONUMENTS

A Disappointment—The Nightingale Group—Sir Francis Vere—Foley's Earl Canning—The Statesmen's Corner—The Fawcett Tablet—Pitt and Fox—Sir Cloudesley Shovel—The Great Clothing Question—The Norris Monument—Wilberforce—Watt—Newton—Stanhope—Wolfe —Chapel of Henry VII.

THE monuments in Westminster Abbey have at least three points of interest about them. They may be regarded from the artistic side. They may be associated with great names. They may be remarkable for the epitaphs upon them. If we take the first of these points we shall arrive shortly at a very disheartening conclusion. Regarded as a museum of monumental sculpture of the highest quality, the Abbey falls very far below what we might have expected of it. A person who had never entered the church, but who had been told that it contained the best sculpture of every English age since the time of Henry III., would come with the highest anticipations, and would assuredly go away disappointed. We have to search for what is good. It does not present itself spontaneously. The royal tombs have been described in an earlier chapter, and need not be mentioned again ; so, too, we have examined the three ancient examples of combined heraldry and sculpture in the chancel, and the effigy and shield of William Valence.

But in addition to these and the others of the same period, there are not many monuments which we can unreservedly praise, and a great number which we cannot but regard with dislike. There are some fifty portrait statues in the church, and upwards of sixty recumbent effigies, and of all that immense number it would be safe to say that not more than a tithe is worthy of the situation. Among the tombs of the Elizabethan and Stuart periods there is much delicate ornament and high finish, but the figures for the most part are clumsily designed. In the next period the figures are better, but less attention is paid to congruity, and some of the sculptures are too obviously out of place. The most remarkable of these is in St. Michael's Chapel. This is Roubiliac's famous group representing Death bursting from the doors of the tomb and attacking with his dart a fainting female by whose side a male figure endeavours in vain to ward off the blow. The figures represent Lady Elizabeth (Shirley), and her husband, Joseph Gascoigne Nightingale; and though the skill of the sculptor is indubitable, we can say little for his taste. Such a monument might have looked better in St. Paul's. Here it has a distracting and disturbing effect, and goes far to destroy the solemnity of all that is around it. There are several other pieces of sculpture by Roubiliac in the church, but this is the most ambitious, and in its own way the most successful. Close to Lady Elizabeth Nightingale's tomb is a very different piece of work, one which, though it is not in strict accordance with the architecture of the church, still is not offensively incongruous. This is the tomb of Sir Francis Vere, one of the little band of Elizabethan heroes who fought so bravely in the Low Countries. A somewhat similar design exists in the church at Breda, where it commemorates Engelbert, count of Nassau. Vere himself, and probably his widow, Elizabeth Dent, who had the monument

I

placed here, must have often seen it. The design is of the
simplest. On a thick slab of black marble lies the effigy of
the deceased knight, while four figures in armour support a
smaller slab on which are his plumed helmet, his breastplate,
and his gauntlets. The figures are very life-like, and were
much admired by Roubiliac, who professed to believe that one
of them was about to speak. The name of the artist of this
admirable monument seems to be unknown.

These two, so close together, excel all the other statues
in force and skill. In seeking for a third monument which
might be classed with them, the eye may, perhaps, be
attracted by Foley's very dignified and graceful statue of
Earl Canning. It is surrounded by many similar portraits
of statesmen, but easily distances its competitors. Foley
showed with consummate ease that modern costume might
be artistically treated; and that, in short, it was the artist
who had to be picturesque much more than the dress. We
have only to compare this figure with that of Peel, executed
by Gibson, to see at a glance the superiority of Foley's
taste. The Peel statue has a certain force and dignity, but
we cannot regret that it is the last in which a statesman
wears a Roman toga. A very typical 'Queen Anne' monument is that designed by Gibbs, the architect of St. Mary-le-
Strand, for the tomb of the Duke of Newcastle. The figures
by Bird are poor enough, but the architectural design, albeit
wholly incongruous, is extremely pleasing. There is much
ambitious sculpture in what has been called 'The Statesmen's
Corner,' but very little of it, regarded simply from an artistic
point of view, deserves even a passing mention. There are
two or three figures by Chantrey which make us wonder at
his great reputation. Bacon's statue of Chatham is rather
good, and very much better than that of Chatham's son

THE THREE CANNINGS.

over the western door. It is one of the first attempts to
employ a modern costume. A very pleasing tablet has been
erected to the memory of a late lamented statesman in a
place so dark that it can seldom be adequately examined.
This is the Abbot's Chapel or Baptistery. Mr. Gilbert
has chosen bronze for the material of the Henry Fawcett
memorial, and the exquisite little allegorical figures which
adorn it are the best of their kind since the little angels
were placed on the tomb of Queen Philippa. When we
look round this chapel and see the statue of Mr. Secretary
Craggs, for which Pope wrote the equivocal lines, beginning—

> 'Statesman, yet friend to truth! of soul sincere,
> In action faithful and in honour clear!'

and the funny little white busts on brackets, of more or less
ornate design, of Keble, Kingsley, and Maurice, we feel
that the force of incongruity can no further go. Craggs is
buried in one of the aisles of the Chapel of Henry VII., as
far as possible from his monument. But Fawcett, Keble,
Kingsley, and Maurice are all buried in country churchyards.

Much has been made of the monuments, not far apart,
of William Pitt and Charles James Fox. Pitt's figure, as
Dean Stanley has observed, seems to dominate the nave.
Its colossal nine feet of white marble must have looked
ghostly indeed when the figure was first put up, and the
stone was still fresh. It was commissioned under a Parliamentary vote, and was completed by Westmacott in 1813.
Nearly ten years elapsed before the same artist finished the
monument of Charles James Fox, though he and Pitt had
died in the same year, 1806. Dean Stanley falls into a
slight error in speaking of these great rivals. 'There is,'
he says, 'but one entry in the register between the burial

of Pitt and the burial of Fox.' Unfortunately, the publication of the complete register by Colonel Chester shows that there are no fewer than five intervening entries. Scott's well-known couplet in ' Marmion ' refers not to the monuments but to the graves. Both were buried in the north transept :—

> ' Drop upon Fox's grave the tear,
> 'Twill trickle to his rival's bier.'

These lines were written years before the two monuments were set up, and still longer before that of Fox had been removed from its original place near the choir in the north transept, to stand where it does now, near the western door.

We have drifted away from artistic monuments to look at those of great statesmen, but it is, I fear, only too true that the more we examine these and the other sculptured memorials here, the less we can admire them. To enjoy the monuments of Westminster Abbey, we must put our taste aside, and go in for historical association and sentiment. Not far from Fox's monument we come to that of a prominent, if not very eminent statesman, Perceval, who is chiefly remembered now for his tragical end. The sculptor, the elder Westmacott, has wrestled unsuccessfully with a difficult subject. There are many of these ' subject sculptures' in the abbey. Nearly all are failures. Tom Thynne being murdered in his coach, André being hanged, ships at sea in an action, and many other such-like scenes, are all in execrable taste, and for the most part in a poor style of sculpture. It is impossible to dwell on them with any pleasure. Let us quote Brayley's account of the monument to Sir Cloudesley Shovel, and make it suffice as an example of the kind of sculpture which Bird, Read, Rysbrack, and others so plentifully bestowed upon the old walls, cutting away ruthlessly the exquisite diaper work, the early arcading, and nearly all that remained of the Crusaders' shields :—

'The monument of that brave officer, Sir Cloudesley Shovel, Knt., who by his abilities and skill raised himself from a very humble station to the rank of Rear-Admiral of Great Britain, is an inelegant though costly structure of various coloured marbles. It consists of an extended basement upon which, between two Corinthian columns and as many pilasters upon each side, is a clumsy marble figure of the deceased, reclining on a sarcophagus, under a dome-like canopy, surmounted by his crest, and having drapery pendant in festoons below. He is absurdly habited in Roman armour, partly covered by a large mantle, which is fastened by a fibula on his right shoulder, and wrapped over his legs and thighs ; to complete the extravagance of this costume he has on a huge periwig, with flowing curls. Two small figures of winged boys or genii, holding shields of arms, are seated on the cornice over the pillars ; and they had formerly trumpets, which have long been destroyed. Within the central pannel of the basement is sculptured a large bas-relief of the Association, the Admiral's ship, striking on the rocks of Scilly (called the Bishop and his Clerks), together with several others of his fleet which were wrecked at the same time. The side pannels contain corresponding groups of various naval trophies.'

Brayley's account of Bird's failure to be picturesque, even with a Roman toga, a fibula, a shipwreck, and a periwig, sets one thinking on the conditions of picturesqueness in sculpture. It is hardly possible to imagine a more suitable place than Westminster Abbey in which to apply any rules we may be able to formulate in our minds on so difficult a subject. The artists who have wrought here have, we may be certain, done their best. If it is the ambition of a hero to win a grave, it is also the ambition of a sculptor to make a monument in Westminster Abbey. No theory that I am acquainted with will account for the number and completeness of the failures. In the one question of costume it may be possible, however, to find some kind of reason for the incompetence of the artists. Unfortunately, though it may account for what we all deplore, it in noways offers us a remedy. A modern sculptor sees a young mower by a river's bank, in a common straw hat and a pair of breeches. A foreign artist naturalised among us sees a farmer in a smock guiding an ox. Phidias saw the Athenian ladies in their linen dresses seated side by side. The unknown carver of the great figure in diorite of Chafra saw Pharaoh himself before him, and makes him look like Pharaoh, though he has only a kilt round his loins and a kerchief on his head. But when Bird, and Read, and a round dozen more whom we will not name, who have disfigured Westminster Abbey with their works, come face to face with the great clothing question, they are struck dumb. Their right hand forgets its cunning. If we look back from them to the great works in the Abbey, to the Nightingale monument— which I do not profess to admire—to the 'hearse' of Sir Francis Vere, to the impressive figures of Queen Elizabeth and Queen Mary Stuart, to Henry VII. and his mother, to the venerable Edward, and the graceful Eleanor, what do we see? Why, that in each case the sculptor has accepted the costume of the day, and has made the most of it. True, Mr. Nightingale is in a dressing-gown and Lady Elizabeth in a peignoir, Sir Francis Vere is wrapped in a cloak, and the royal personages wear royal robes. But there are many other examples to which we may appeal in order to prove that the inability to make contemporary costume picturesque is inherent not in the costume but in the artist : and the old proverb which makes a bad carpenter complain of his tools, applies with equal force to the sculptor who complains that the costume of his own day is unsuited for artistic treatment.

Take, for example, the Norris monument in the Chapel of St. Andrew. Henry, Lord Norris was one of the few persons on whom Queen Elizabeth conferred a peerage. He owed it, no doubt, partly to the firmness of his father, Sir Henry, who was hanged at Tyburn, denying with his last breath the guilt of Anne Boleyn. Lord Norris and his wife are finely sculptured in alabaster, he in armour, and his wife in her robes of state, both with their heads resting on embroidered cushions and their hands raised as if in prayer. On the basement are their six sons—six heroes of the Elizabethan wars, of whose great deeds the annals of Irish rebellion are very full. All of them died or were killed before their parents, except one. 'They all appear as praying,' says Brayley, 'except the youngest on the north side, who is looking upward, with features highly expressive of amenity and cheerfulness, his right hand being spread open on his breast, and his left resting upon his hip. This is the best executed statue of the whole; from the difference of the expression and attitude it would seem to have been intended for the surviving son.'

As a contrast to successful work like the Norris statues, we may look at the figure of William Wilberforce, by Joseph, in the north aisle of the choir. It has contemporary costume, and must be a likeness; but if so, it is only in so far as the lamented Carlo Pellegrini's caricatures were likenesses. The artist, instead of at least attempting to impart some dignity to the figure of a man who, whatever his narrowness and other shortcomings, was undoubtedly great, has picked out only characteristics which a true artist would have omitted or softened down, and has adopted those tricks of expression, manner, and attitude, which make this one of the most unpleasant, and indeed ludicrous, figures in the Abbey.

Another and very typical example of how not to use contemporary costume is afforded by the gigantic statue of

Watt, which was with difficulty and widespread destruction of other memorials dragged into the Chapel of St. Paul. It is only a cenotaph—the great engineer was buried at Birmingham. It is, I had almost said, a flagrant, but certainly a conspicuous example of the false standard of high art which was taught and practised by Chantrey, Haydon, and others of that time. The design is one which would hardly have been tolerable in miniature. Magnified to its enormous proportions it is simply a nightmare, empty in all that makes sculpture great except that least valuable quality of mere hugeness.

Still searching for examples of good sculpture, we may mention a few other monuments, reserving the epitaphs for a future chapter. The two most conspicuous of all, as seen from the west door of the nave, are those of Newton and Stanhope on either side of the entrance to the choir. Stanhope is not buried here, but Newton lies immediately in front of the monument, which was designed by Kent and executed by Rysbrach, and is not very bad. It includes a sarcophagus on which reclines a figure of Sir Isaac looking at two Cupids, who seem to set him a mathematical problem. From a pyramid in the background a globe projects, with Astronomy personified by a female figure seated upon it. The globe is covered with constellations, and shows the path of a comet as calculated in 1680 by Newton. Below are groups of children engaged in philosophical transactions, and weighing the sun and moon with a steel-yard. Nothing can really be more absurd than the crowding of allegory upon allegory in this extraordinary composition. Besides Newton himself his pretty but naughty niece was buried in the Abbey. After the death of Lord Halifax, who is said to have been her lover, and who by the way was also buried in the Abbey, she married John Conduitt, Master of the Mint, and both she and her husband are buried beside her famous uncle, Sir Isaac, in the middle aisle. With them also was interred the body of her daughter, Lady Lymington.

The corresponding monument to Newton's is that of Stanhope, on the southern side of the choir entrance. It is of very similar design, the great general being represented in a Roman costume, attended by Victory and other emblematical figures.

Close to the two masterpieces—Roubiliac's Lady Elizabeth Nightingale and the anonymous monument of Sir Francis Vere—is one of the worst of the many failures to be found within these walls. Although General Wolfe was killed at Quebec in 1759, the monument was not finished till 1772. The sculptor, Joseph Wilton, was wholly unequal to the task committed to his hands, and he had no Wren or Kent or Gibbs to make the architectural part of his design. The result is bald, ill-composed, and ungraceful to a degree unparalleled elsewhere. The great clothing question of which I have already spoken becomes acute in Wilson's case, and he fairly breaks down before it. He seems, in fact, to have wholly lost his head when he came to deal with it. Wolfe is actually represented as nude. Over him stoops a grenadier in full uniform, and above him hovers a female figure clothed in a classical dress, and supposed to represent Victory. The result is absurdity and confusion, not lessened by the introduction of a highlander, of a couple of very tame lions, and of a wolf's head on a shield.

Beside the Royal tombs already mentioned, the Chapel of Henry VII. contains some interesting and a few handsome monuments. At the eastern end of the north aisle, beyond the tomb of Queen Elizabeth, are three children's memorials.

MONUMENT OF DEAN STANLEY.

In the centre is a marble vase or urn, of fine design, made
by Sir Christopher Wren, 1678, for the reception of portions
of two small skeletons which some workmen had found, four
years before, when cutting through a wall under the chapel
in the White Tower. It was reasonably believed that these
were the bones of the two sons of Edward IV., who
mysteriously disappeared during the usurpation of Richard III.
The boy king, Edward V., it will be remembered, was actually
born in the Sanctuary of Westminster Abbey, when his mother
took refuge here while her husband was fighting for his
crown in 1471. On either side of the marble urn is a small
monument to a daughter of James I. The Princess Sophia
was but three days old at the time of her death in 1606.
She is represented as an infant in a cradle. The marble has
turned very brown, but when it was fresh and white it may
have been possible to admire the carving intended to represent
point-lace. The Princess Mary died in 1607, and her effigy
reclines on a small altar tomb. It is hardly superior as a work
of art to the cradle of her little sister, and neither figure does
much credit to the sculptor, Maximilian Powtrain.

In the southern aisle, besides the monuments already
mentioned, the most remarkable object is the great, but
uninscribed, memorial of General Monk, designed by Kent
and carved by Scheemakers. Although he died in 1670 it
was not put up till 1720.

The large and ugly group of allegorical figures which fills
up the first of the five apsidal chapels, contrasts curiously with
the two effigies in the next recess. It commemorates the last
members of the Lennox family, including the lovely lady
whose figure, as Britannia, still appears upon our coinage.
In the adjoining chapel, beside Sir J. Boehm's recumbent
statue of Dean Stanley already mentioned, there is a fairly

satisfactory figure, by Westmacott, of the Duke of Montpensier, a brother of Louis-Philippe, who died an exile in England in 1807, and is here interred. In the opposite chapel, on the north side to that of the Lennox family on the south, is the vault of the Villiers family, and the huge monument which commémorates both the Dukes of Buckingham, who were buried under it. The adjoining monument of Sheffield, duke of Buckingham (properly of Normanby and Bucking-hamshire), is more remarkable for the inscription it bears than for its sculpture, and may best be reserved for another chapter.

THE EPITAPHS

Absence of interesting Epitaphs—Feckenham's Texts—The Duchess of Gloucester—Queen Elizabeth—Chaucer—Bourchier—Lord Russell—Sir Samuel Morland—John Smith—Poets' Corner—Garrick—Handel—Drayton—Johnson—Goldsmith—Thomas Smith—William Laurence—The 'Loyall Duke'—The Texts—Fairborne—Buckingham—Prior—Atterbury—Newton—Boulter.

IT is a curious fact that though the church contains the inscribed tombs of the many generations of Englishmen eminent in politics, war, literature, religion, and the arts, the number of the epitaphs worth repeating for their own sakes does not exceed half-a-dozen.

Westminster Abbey is justly famous for beautiful and stately tombs of the Elizabethan and Jacobean periods. In spite of 'restoration,' by which in the past fifty years such tombs have been decimated in country churches, they still abound; and, after their beautiful design, they are chiefly remarkable for quaint inscriptions, generally in excellent English—the English of Shakespeare's day—and for the curious verbal conceits, often descending into mere puns on names, which were the fashion at that time. No part of England is without them except Westminster. They abound in London, where we see them in all the city churches. They are common in Middlesex, Essex, Kent, Hertfordshire, and Surrey. But whether the awe which affected men's minds *in loco terribili*, or whether there was no scholar or poet at hand, as in many a country parish, Westminster Abbey is singularly destitute of epitaphs of what, so far as regards the rest of England, may be considered the great epitaph-making period; one or two in the cloisters do but prove the rule. If we hark back it is just the same. The words already quoted as having been painted by Feckenham on the tomb of Edward I. are the most stirring of those which belong to the Reformation period. Some of the royal tombs have, or have had, rhyming Latin inscriptions, of which Camden and other antiquaries have given us the texts,—remarkable chiefly for the excruciating treatment of quantity by which they are pervaded. One or two examples will be found below; but, with the exception of a few words on the monument of Richard II., but probably, as we shall see, later than his time, there is hardly a trace of pathos or poetry in any of them. It is the same with the epitaphs of lesser folk. The few heroes and bishops and kings' cousins who are buried in the chapels have curt inscriptions over them in bad Latin prose. Of a later period than the Elizabethan and Stuart, of the time of the Revolution and downwards through the eighteenth century, the number of extant epitaphs increases largely, but the quality remains the same. Nor has it improved down to our own time. Some great men and great poets have assayed to write suitable lines for the grave of a departed worthy; but when I say that the poor verses by Lord Tennyson on Franklin are the best of this period, it will be seen that I have failed to find anything I can praise. Lord Tennyson's lines are as follows :—

'Not here : the White North has thy bones ; and thou,
        Heroic sailor soul,
    Art passing on thy happier voyage now
        Towards no earthly pole.'

The last line is peculiarly awkward and obscure, to my mind, but the epitaph has many admirers, and, at least, it is no worse than Pope's on Kneller. Perhaps some adaptations of texts are the best, where an eminent preacher has known what would be a suitable quotation from the Bible to add to the names and dates on a stone. Epitaph-writing is a lost art; and even when it flourished made few signs of its existence visible in the Abbey church of Westminster, and — I had almost said, naturally—those in the Poets' Corner are the worst, perhaps because they are the most disappointing.

It seems odd that some little sentences of Feckenham's should have deceived antiquaries and historians almost to our own day. The tomb of the wife of Edward I. is remarkable for a French inscription, and has also Feckenham's tag 'DISCE MORI,' scarcely visible now. The text to the tomb of Edward III. is of the same character, but is not now visible :—

'PUGNA PRO PATRIA.'

The rhyming Latin verses are still round the edge of the metal table on which the effigy lies. They consist of only six lines, of which the last, and by no means the worst, may be taken as a specimen :—

'Armipotens rexit—jam cœlo Cœlice Rex sit.'

NORTH AISLE OF THE CHOIR.

K

The adjoining tomb of Queen Philippa has no inscription, but Feckenham painted on it :—

'Conjux Edwardi jacet hic Regina Philippa.
DISCE VIVERE.'

The great tomb of Richard II. and Anne of Bohemia still bears its epitaph, one line of which only need be inflicted on the reader :—

' Obruit hereticos—et corum stravit amicos.'

On this tomb Feckenham placed the one pathetic line to be found in the Chapel of the Kings :—

'FUISSE FAELICEM MISERRIMUM.'

He put on the queen's tomb :—

'FORMA FRAGILIS.'

And on that of Henry V. :—

'DOMAT OMNIA VIRTUS.'

The last of these sentences which need be mentioned was on a tablet to commemorate Katherine, Henry's widow :—

'OTIUM FUGE.'

This, I think, exhausts the list of Feckenham's efforts for the puzzle of posterity—most successful efforts, as any one can testify who has waded through all the futile guesses bestowed on 'Pactum Serva.' By the way, 'Forma Fragilis' is prettily translated by Camden as 'Favour Fadeth.'

The epitaphs on Edward III. and Richard II. are of a very rare class. Indeed, I doubt if any other fourteenth century rhyming Latin inscriptions of the kind have come down to

us. There are no others in the Abbey. The Duchess of
Gloucester lies in the Chapel of St. Edmund, under the fine
brass already mentioned, and much of her epitaph may still
be read ; but it is in a very different style, being merely her
name and titles, and the names and titles of her father and
her husband, with the date of her death, 1389, all in French.

The inscription on the monument of Queen Elizabeth comes
next in order. The universal grief of the nation at her death
is set forth, and a list is given of her triumphs—of the establishment of the Protestant religion, her reform of the coinage,
and her personal accomplishments ; 'but,' to quote the words
of Dean Stanley, 'the most pathetic record which survives is
to be found in the two lines at the head of the monument,
inscribed by James I. with a deeper feeling than we should
naturally have ascribed to him :—"Regno consortes et urnâ,
hic obdormimus Elizabetha et Maria sorores, in spe resurrectionis." The long war of the English Reformation is closed
in those words. The sisters are at one ; the daughter of
Catherine of Arragon and the daughter of Anne Boleyn rest
in peace.'

We must not pass by some other inscriptions of Tudor times.
William Caxton, the printer, set up on a pillar a tablet near
the grave of Geoffrey Chaucer. Mr. Blades appears to have
thought Caxton set up the pillar as well as the tablet, but it
is evident from his own words that the tablet was hung to
a neighbouring column. He 'lieth buried tofore the chapel
of Seynte Benet ; by whos sepulture is wreton on a table
honging on a pylere his Epitaphye maad by a Poete Laureat.'
Stephen Surigo of Milan was the poet laureate who wrote the
'epitaphy,' which is to be found in Caxton's edition of Chaucer's
translation of Boethius. There was no other memorial of
Chaucer here till Nicholas Brigham, in the reign of Queen

Mary, made the Gothic tomb still extant, with a new epitaphy
which has perished. Camden gives us a copy of it, but it
is not worth reprinting. Brigham, at all events, did not
celebrate his own name except in a single line at the end,
unlike Benson, who set up Milton's tablet, with a short sentence
about Milton and a long one about himself. Humphrey
Bourchier, who was buried near his ancestress, the Duchess of
Gloucester, was the eldest son of Lord Berners, and father of
the second lord, who made that delightful translation of
Froissart's 'Chronicle.' He was killed on the fateful Easter
Sunday at Barnet which decided the fate of Henry VI.; and
partly, no doubt, because he had followed the flag of the
victorious Edward, but partly also, we may suppose, on account
of his illustrious descent, he was buried in the Chapel of St.
Edmund. His fine heraldic brass has already been mentioned,
or, at least, what remains of it. The inscription, like the effigy,
has disappeared, but Camden preserved a copy of it, and if it
really was on the tomb, and not merely 'honging on a pylere,'
will have offered an early example of unrhymed quantitative
Latin verse. The last two lines may suffice as a specimen :—

> 'Armis conspicuus quondam charusque Britannis
> Hic fuit ; ut cœlis vivat deposcite votis.'

If these verses are contemporary, which I strongly doubt,
they are a little earlier than the time of Caxton, and show the
Renascence influence to which the art of printing gave such
an impetus. In an adjoining inscription in the same chapel
we may see how far this influence carried epitaph-makers. It
commemorates Lord Russell, the eldest son and heir of the
second Earl of Bedford ; and Brayley, in the language of sixty
years ago, tells us that he left a widow, 'whose excessive grief
at his loss is elegantly described in several inscriptions

composed by herself in Greek, Latin, and English.' As Lord
Russell died in 1584, this is almost certainly the first introduction of a Greek epitaph to the Abbey. Lady Russell was
one of the learned daughters of Sir Anthony Cook of Gidea
Hall. A specimen of the English verses will be enough
here :—

> 'Right noble twice, by virtue and by birth,
> Of Heaven loved and honoured on the earth.'

The Elizabethan epitaphs still extant are very numerous, but
very uninteresting for the most part. They are chiefly in
Latin, and of a pronounced classical character ; almost, and
in some cases quite, heathen in sentiment. The gods and
goddesses of old Rome and the Muses of Greece are invoked ;
and this tendency becomes more and more marked as time
goes on. The bilingual and trilingual epitaphs are outdone by
the monuments erected in the nave late in the seventeenth
century by Sir Samuel Morland, to the memory of his wives,
the first of whom died in 1674, and the second in 1680. The
inscriptions are in Hebrew, Greek, and Ethiopic, the only
English parts being the names and dates. When we have
spelled them out—for I assume that my readers are as well
acquainted as I am myself with these familiar languages,—we
may turn for a moment to a very pleasing design, in the
Palladian style, by Gibbs. It is the monument of one John
Smith—that most English of names could not fail to appear in
the Abbey—and the epitaph, which is dated in 1718, contains
the well-known line about Mr. Smith's origin, ' Prosapia
Smithorum Lincolniensium oriundus.'

We may next look into Poets' Corner, and try to find
something worthy of the great names we see around us.
Taking the monuments in topographical order, we come first

to David Garrick, buried here in 1779. The figure is, literally, theatrical, and the verses, which bear the unfamiliar name of Pratt, are worthy of it. Charles Lamb characterised them as 'a farrago of false thoughts and nonsense.' Nearly as absurd is the monument of the learned Grabe, called in his epitaph 'Grabus' (d. 1711), who is represented sitting on his own coffin. It is by Bird; but in this transept, and on this west wall, it is surprising to see such great names so ill represented. Rysbrack's Gay, Nollekens' Goldsmith, Marshall's Campbell, the second Duke of Argyll, by Roubiliac, are all extremely poor, but all distanced by Roubiliac's Handel. But we are too easily tempted to wander from the epitaphs to the statues. Handel fares better in this respect than most of his neighbours. The text he so splendidly illustrated by the music of his 'Messiah,' 'I know that my Redeemer liveth,' is inscribed with the notes on an open page before him, and below we see nothing but his name and age. On the east side, which consists only of a wall one bay wide, are the monuments, cenotaphs, of Shakespeare, Burns, and Southey, none of them buried here; while on the south wall are monuments to Jonson, Spenser, Butler, Milton, Gray, and Thomson. On the outer side of the screen are memorials to Granville Sharp, the philanthropist, and to Matthew Prior. It seems rather odd to say, that though a more or less lengthy epitaph is appended to each of these (except one, that of 'Rare Ben Jonson'), I do not find, after careful search, anything worth quoting from them. The eastern aisle of the Poets' Corner contains some of the most famous monuments, but so far as inscriptions can be called ornamental, those are best adorned which are not adorned at all. The lines on Drayton would be fine if they were appropriate. They are attributed both to Quarles and to Ben Jonson, and are certainly very like the work of the last-

named, though it is not sublime, but ridiculous, to tell the
'pious marble' that when its ruins cease to commemorate
Drayton,

'His name, that cannot fade, shall be
An everlasting monument to thee.'

After a brief survey of these epitaphs, and having with
difficulty suppressed one's disgust at the odious little busts
of Archbishop Tait, Longfellow, Grote, Thirlwall, Macaulay,
and Thackeray—which seem, so are they arranged, to be
playing at hide-and-seek behind the columns—we may note
with satisfaction the simple grave of Dr. Johnson, with only
the date of his death and his age on it, and may look up
at Goldsmith's tablet over the Revestry Door, just above.
Johnson, who thought an epitaph ought to be in Latin,
himself wrote the inscription.   It contains the well-known
and oft-quoted sentences, 'Qui nullum ferè scribendi genus
non tetigit, nullum tetigit quod non ornavit.'

The graves of Sheridan, Campbell, and Dickens are on
the floor, Dickens wholly lost in the glory of his surroundings.
He should have been buried, as he himself desired, at
Rochester, where his grave would have been an object of
pilgrimage.   Here he is a little more than nobody.

As it would manifestly be absurd to attempt a systematic
account of all the curiosities of 'epitaphy' (or shall we say
'epitaphigraphy'?) in the Abbey, we had best choose a few
examples here and there as worthy of more than a moment's
delay.   Far away in the Infirmary Cloister we should notice
a tablet in the north walk, to the memory of Mr. Thomas
Smith, who died in 1664, and 'through the spotted vaile
of the small-pox rendered a pure and unspotted soul to
God.'   In the east cloister is an affecting epitaph on a little
girl, dated in 1680.   'Jane Lister.   Deare Child.'

There is one epitaph of the seventeenth century in the church which retains something of this character. It is a fine monument in the north transept, erected to commemorate William Cavendish, described as 'the Loyall Duke of Newcastle,' who died in 1676, and his wife, who died in 1673, and of whom we read that she was a wise and learned lady, as 'her many bookes do well testifie' (her life of the duke, her husband, is still read), and that she was the 'youngest sister to the Lord Lucas, of Colchester, a noble familie, for all the Brothers were Valiant, and all the Sisters Virtuous.' This sentence is often quoted, but seldom ascribed to an epitaph in Westminster Abbey by an anonymous writer of the seventeenth century. In the centre of the nave we encounter some of the best of the Scriptural texts alluded to above. Over the grave of Field-Marshal Pollock (1872) is this very appropriate quotation from the hundred and fortieth Psalm :—'O God the Lord, the strength of my salvation, Thou hast covered my head in the day of battle.' This offers a curious contrast to the bloodthirsty sentiments expressed by the widowéd Lady Fairborne in a tablet on the opposite wall. Sir Palmes Fairborne had been governor of Tangier, and was killed in 1680 by the Moors. The verses on the monument should be noticed in any case as having been written by Dryden; but three couplets must suffice :—

'The Candian siege his early valour knew,
Where Turkish blood did his young hands embrue.

More bravely British general never fell,
Nor general's death was e'er avenged so well.
Which his pleased eyes beheld before their close,
Followed by a thousand victims of his foes.'

Things did not improve much in a century, as a still more bloodthirsty epitaph, a little further east upon the same wall, dated 1782, clearly proves. But to return to the texts. One of these, on the grave of Livingstone, has always been considered most appropriate since it was placed here by Dean Stanley :—'Other sheep I have which are not of this fold.' Over Sir Charles Barry's grave is (Col. iii. 23, 24, beginning), 'And whatsoever ye do, do it heartily.'

A very curious epitaph, and one about which much has been written, is that of the Duke of Buckingham in the Chapel of Henry VII. The duke died in 1721 in February, and another great man, of less illustrious rank and descent, in September of the same year. This was Matthew Prior, who is buried close to Spenser's monument, and who mocked at ancestry in the famous lines :—

> 'Nobles and Heralds, by your leave
> Here lies what once was Matthew Prior :
> A son of Adam and of Eve :
> Can Bourbon or Nassau go higher?'

When Matthew Prior was English minister at the court of Louis XIV., the bust here seen was sculptured by Coysevox and presented to the poet by the King. Prior was naturally pleased at the compliment, and, as he says in his will, 'for this last piece of human vanity' bequeathed the bust to be made part of a monument to his memory, permitting his executors to spend 500l. upon the design, and leaving these lines to be placed under his name :—

> 'To me 'tis given to die, to you 'tis given
> To live : alas ! one moment sets us even :
> Mark how impartial is the will of Heaven.'

Atterbury was at this time Dean of Westminster and Bishop of Rochester. In religious matters he was probably a very free thinker, though nominally a High Churchman, and in

any case a man of strong views and opinions, who eventually
went into exile for the house of Stuart, and ended his days
abroad.   But while he held the office of Dean he was
tyrannical as to epitaphs.   They must be in Latin, and might
be as heathenish as possible.   Christianity was to be rigidly
excluded.   Atterbury himself, especially in his later years of
exile, showed a Christian spirit in many ways.   Why he
looked on Westminster Abbey church as a heathen temple,
a kind of Pantheon, I do not know.   But his view as to
epitaphs certainly seems to have been this : an epitaph ought
to be in Latin : the best Latin is not Christian, but heathen,
or at least pre-Christian : therefore the epitaphs to be inscribed
on the walls of Westminster must contain as little Christianity
and as little religion of any kind as possible.   All which is,
no doubt, very consistent, but hardly satisfies us as the
appropriate attitude of the dean of a Christian church.   The
result of his views may be seen both on the monument of
Matthew Prior and on that of the Duke of Buckingham.
Prior's pretty little English triplet was absolutely rejected.
Atterbury wrote at the time of Prior's death that he would
do as he had promised regarding his tomb, 'particularly as
to the triplet he wrote for his own epitaph, which, while we
were on good terms, I promised him should never appear on
his tomb while I was Dean of Westminster.'   Dr. Freind
accordingly wrote a long classical Latin inscription, which
does not contain a single interesting line, and which carefully
avoids even the slightest allusion to the fact that it was composed for the walls of a Christian church, and to mark the
grave of a man who, whatever his shortcomings, had been
baptized into the Christian faith.

The case of Buckingham's epitaph goes on all fours with
this of Prior's.   The duke, certainly of all men of his day,

represented every kind of culture, including the most pedantic
study of the classics. He wrote for his own epitaph what
every one who has read it in its complete form must consider
a touching and beautiful prayer, expressive rather of trembling
hope than of confident faith, but perhaps none the less
Christian on that account. It runs as follows :—

> 'Dubius, sed non improbus, vixi ;
> Incertus morior, non perturbatus ;
> Humanum est nescire et errare :
> *Christum adveneror*, Deo confido
> Omnipotente Benevolentissime ;
> Ens entium, miserere mei.'

Even John Newton admired the last line. I must refer to
Dean Stanley's remarks on the whole subject. They are very
interesting and delicately critical, and I merely pause to
observe that Atterbury struck out the words put in italic
above.

Two other epitaphs of the same century can hardly be
passed by. Sir Isaac Newton, whose somewhat extravagant
monument was described in the last chapter, died in March
1727 as we reckon it, but the Old Style 1726 is on his tomb-
stone. The epitaph on the monument is, to say the least,
disappointing. The death of such a man called forth from
the poets of the day some very fair verses. Johnson severely
criticises the inscription as it is. A long catalogue of his
discoveries, 'which no philosopher can want, and which none
but a philosopher can understand,' is his verdict. Pope wrote
some lines which were never set up ; they are too extravagant
in their eulogy, and have a 'made-to-order' ring which is
unpleasing :—

> 'Nature and Nature's laws lay hid in night :
> God said, "*Let Newton be!*" and all was light.'

It is a pity, perhaps, that a few lines could not have been
selected from Thomson's 'Poem Sacred to the Memory of
Sir Isaac Newton,' which seems to me the finest of these
numerous elegies.   In it occur the well-known lines referring
to the rainbow and the prismatic colours :—

> ' Did ever poet image aught so fair,
> Dreaming in whispering groves by the hoarse brook,
> Or Prophet, to whose rapture Heaven descends?'

And those on Newton's chronological investigations :—

> ' The noiseless tide of Time, all bearing down
> To vast Eternity's unbounded Sea,
> Where the green islands of the happy shine,
> He stemmed alone.'

The last sentence should not be omitted :—

> ' While in expectance of the second life,
> When Time shall be no more, thy sacred dust
> Sleeps with her Kings, and dignifies the scene.'

The last epitaph I shall notice is nearly contemporary.
Archbishop Boulter died in 1742.   He was alternately the
friend and the enemy of Dean Swift, and was during a
considerable part of his life virtually governor of Ireland under
successive Lords-Lieutenant.   His principle of action may be
briefly summed up—'Ireland for the English.'   As may be
imagined, his life was anything but a placid one, and the
contrast is grim between the reality and the pious fiction of
the epitaph, which after recounting his virtues in very
commonplace language ends thus: 'He was born January
the 4th, 1671 : he was consecrated Bishop of Bristol, 1718 :
he was translated to the Archbishopric of Armagh, 1723; and
from thence to Heaven, September the 27th, 1742.'

A WALK IN THE PRECINCTS

A Benedictine Monastery—The Domestic Buildings—Gradual Growth of the Church—The North Transept—Sir Christopher Wren—The Western Towers—Great and Little Dean's Yard—Ashburnham House —The old Dormitory—Burlington's Dormitory—The College Garden —College Street—The Abbey as a *Campo Santo*—Conclusion.

A BENEDICTINE monastery, or, in fact, any monastery of the old foundation, whether it professed the reformed Benedictine rule or not, was built almost always on the same plan. The arrangement of the 'house' as distinguished from the 'church' varied but little where the exigencies of the site did not demand unusual treatment. At Westminster, as at St. Albans—the only other English monastery to compete with it in size and importance—the domestic buildings, including the cloisters and the refectory, were on the south side of the church. In a church like St. Paul's, which belonged to secular canons, cloisters and a refectory were not a necessity. The canons did not reside constantly in the domestic buildings; the church was the first thing, and the regular celebration of Divine service was easily provided for when the canon appointed a vicar to take his turn of duty. In a monastery like Westminster the domestic buildings were of prime importance. The smallest part of the service of the church could not be maintained until some accommodation had been provided for the monks. The canons

of St. Paul's could live where they pleased, and there is plenty
of evidence that in the eleventh and twelfth centuries a canon
lived at home with his wife and children, whom in most cases,
no doubt, he left at his country prebendal manor-house when
he took his turn in the cathedral. A community like that of
Westminster was wholly different. The monks shared the
same refectory and dormitory; they were fed from the same
kitchen, and their diet, bread and ale, was prepared on the
premises.

The church of Westminster Abbey was begun in the reign
of Edward the Confessor, and was finished in the reign of
George II. During all that long period its growth was con-
tinuous. Since the so-called Gothic revival became an active
force, successive architects have been endeavouring, with too
much success, to obliterate the marks of that growth; but why
we should accept the opinions of a modern Gothic architect as
to what the church ought to be I do not know, seeing it never
was at any one time as he would have us believe. The north
transept was never in the reign, say, of Richard II. a bit more
like that which has now been built than it was like that built
in 1722 by Wren and his pupils. We are not compelled to
accept either as like the original, and, of course, from the
archaeological and artistic point of view, are inclined to think
the work of Wren's school of a century and a half ago superior
in interest to that of Scott or his disciples at the present day.
In any case, we have allowed a building almost two hundred
years old to be taken away, for no special reason, in favour of
a wholly modern and conjectural design, in a style which was
never much in vogue in England, and least of all at Westminster, and have looked on at the destruction of a rose
window dated 1722.

Sir Christopher reports that the northern transept was out

THE NORTH TRANSEPT.

of repair in 1713, and that he had made a design to restore
it to its proper shape. This design in a curious drawing,
apparently by one of his pupils, was published in the *Building
News* of 26th October, 1888, and shows that Wren's ideas
were not only far ahead of those of the architects of his time,
but also far ahead of those of the architects of our time, even
after the benign influence of fifty years of the great Gothic
revival. It is usual to assert that Wren failed in his Gothic
detail. A good deal might be said on the other side.

The new north front of Westminster Abbey, when the
present scaffolding was cleared away, was found to offend
against every one of the canons of taste which must have
actuated Wren in making the building now being destroyed.

The first consideration with him was, no doubt, the general
outline. In this his marvellous eye for effect, or, to speak
more exactly, his trained mathematical knowledge, gave him a
great advantage. He saw, of course, that elaborate carving
and specious ornament would be out of place in a north front
raising itself one hundred and seventy feet against any daylight
there ever is in a London sky : that outline and mass must be
everything and mere decoration nothing. On this principle he
designed the new north front, with such success that it used to
be one of the most difficult things to believe that the gable end
of the transept was no higher than any other part of the great
cruciform building. This is well seen in a print, with which
many of my readers may be familiar, by C. Wild, published
in 1805, in which the light is well managed and produces just
the right scenic effect.

If instead of entering the church we turn to the westward,
along the north side of the now 'thoroughly restored' nave,
we reach the much-abused towers. How they have escaped
the ravages of the last fifty years is one of those standing

miracles for which it is so hard to account. However, there they are, much as they were left when their architect, assuredly not Wren, who, in fact, was dead a dozen years before, handed them over complete to the Dean and Chapter in 1735. I pointed out in a former chapter the curious fact that the first and last royal tombs are practically in the same style. The exterior of the Abbey, begun in a 'dialect,' so to speak, of Romanesque, by Edward the Confessor, was completed in another dialect of the same style in the reign of George II. These western towers have been often threatened. I trust they will survive a few years longer, by which time a better turn may have taken place in the tide of architectural taste; but it is curious to note that a hundred years after the death of Wren even so accurate an author as Brayley talks of his style—with special reference to these towers—as Grecian.

At this western front we are as nearly as possible where the Almonry and its chapel stood, for in the reign of Edward IV. it must be remembered that the precincts were surrounded with walls, within which were many courts and gardens and other small sub-divisions, most of which have now disappeared. We have still, however, Great and Little Deans' Yards; the picturesque court which gives entrance to the Queen's Scholars' Hall, formerly the Abbot's Refectory; the College Garden, and the small open space behind Ashburnham House.

There is little to detain the visitor in Great Dean's Yard; but one of the best views of the Church is to be had from its south-western corner; and the northern and eastern sides are made up in part of ancient buildings, some cruelly restored, others less cruelly mutilated to fit them for modern habita-. tions. The Head Master's House has been adapted by slow degrees from the lodgings of the Abbey cellarer, and is full

L

of picturesque corners within and without. It contains a marvellous series of portraits of head masters, reaching back to Elizabethan times, and including a very interesting likeness of the great Camden, who was an assistant here and afterwards the only lay head master.

We can enter Little Dean's Yard by a passage close to the Head Master's House. Once within, we see on the left Ashburnham House, one of Inigo Jones's masterpieces; next beyond it an unnecessarily ugly modern house on a foundation as old as anything here ; and at right angles to it the southern extremity of the ancient monastic Dormitory, partly masked and concealed by the well-known porch, carved all over with the names of former scholars. The south side of Little Dean's Yard is occupied by school-buildings of comparatively modern date.

Ashburnham House is so plain outside that a visit to the interior comes as a pleasant surprise. It has been, however, so often described of late that I need do little more here than mention some interesting discoveries of old work which were recently shown to me by the kindness of the Head Master. As is well known, Ashburnham House is built, so to speak, astride of the thick wall of the ancient Misericorde. In making some investigations with a view to discovering the original dimensions of Inigo's hall, which has been much cut up with panelled partitions, Mr. Rutherford found some windows apparently of Litlington's period, and what may safely be identified as a ' buttery hatch,' or aperture communicating with the kitchen of the refectory. We may observe, in passing, that the interior arrangements of Ashburnham House have not been in any way injured since its occupation by the School, and the visitor can still admire the beauty of the spacious staircase and of the chief reception-rooms on the

first floor. The unfortunate third storey, which does so much
to spoil the front, was built by one of the last canons in
occupation.

The old Dormitory of the Monks is as well worthy of a
visit as anything within the ancient precincts. By some
judicious and as many injudicious alterations it has been
converted into a noble hall, where the Head Master can sit
on a kind of throne at one end while his pupils are working
out their papers at separate desks. The roof is of dark
timber, somewhat rough and of uncertain date. The walls
are mainly of the most ancient period, containing arches and
doorways which may well have been placed where they are
by Edward the Confessor. It will be remembered that the
northern end of this same building forms the Chapter library
already described. Before leaving this block of buildings, the
visitor should, if possible, obtain admission to a room sometimes called Dr. Busby's Parlour, formerly a school library,
and still containing some curious books, but now fitted up as
a museum. This chamber, which is charmingly situated with
a window opening on the college gardens, retains its Stuart
features, among which the exquisite plaster-work wreath which
adorns the domed ceiling will be specially admired. Busby
died in 1695. In the view across the garden, from the
window of the museum, a portion of the present dormitory
is seen among the green trees. Strange to say, this is the
most beautiful building of its kind in London, and at the
same time the least known.

We have hardly any relics of Lord Burlington's work left.
The best was, of course, his own house in Piccadilly. It is
significant of the present state of aesthetic culture in England,
that this exquisite building was destroyed for the benefit of
the Royal Academy of Arts. To speak more strictly, it was

destroyed because the so-called architects employed were not
clever or competent enough to make a new design in which
the old one might be preserved, no very difficult task it might
be thought. Lord Burlington rightly thought that in such a
situation—then, no doubt, littlê better than a marsh—the
ground-floor should not be used for habitation, and kept the
lower storey as an open arcade, consisting of fifteen massive
arches. Above is a row of as many niches intended for
statues. Above this again is a row of square windows, and the
building ends with a deep cornice. It is of freestone, now in
parts somewhat decayed, and the lower arcade has been filled
up, the space within being utilised for studies, the modern
drainage and warming arrangements making possible what a
hundred years ago would have been dangerous. From the
simplicity of the elements of this design, as described above, it
will be seen that its beauty does not in any way depend on
ornament. The niches were never filled; there is not a
square inch of carving on the whole surface; there is no
coloured marble, or polished granite, or gilt bronze; yet the
result is perfectly satisfactory and eminently beautiful. I do
not say that the modern architect who covers his shortcomings
with unmeaning friezes and reliefs, and hides his bad construction with rows of vases, and shining knobs of green and
red stone, would be able to see and appreciate rightly the
subtle beauty of such a building as this. On the contrary, he
will probably call it, as a modern architect called the Banquet-
ing House at Whitehall, 'an ugly barn'; and I can only hope
that, as it has lain half hidden for so many years, it may
continue so until the present depression in architectural taste
is a thing of the past.

The interior was never completed, but remains a long, lofty
room divided into 'cubicles,' for the sleeping accommodation

of the forty scholars on the foundation.   It is about 160 feet long and about 30 feet high.

Visitors are not admitted to the College Garden, which belongs to the 'college' as represented by the clergy of the 'collegiate' church and not to the school; but it is not difficult for any one interested to obtain leave to see one of the best views of what remain of the old buildings. We can return through the infirmary cloisters, or, rather, through their site, for the present arcades are very modern, and some of the buildings by which they are flanked are in the most modern, and, among these old relics, distressingly conspicuous style known, and justly, as 'Gothic.'   'Vandal' would suit it as well.   A few steps further, under the low arches of Edward's buildings, and we are back in the Great Cloister.

The visitor should go out through the only precinct gate still remaining, that at the south-eastern corner of Dean's Yard. Here, formerly, was a bridge and a brook, both now far underground ; and the archway, modernised on the inner side, only represents the original gate.   College Street contains some rather picturesque old houses, but is chiefly worth a visit for the view of the Abbey, the School, and the circumjacent buildings which may be obtained from it.

This is not the place in which to suggest improvements on the present system, but I cannot help thinking that something like the ten years' rule which prevails in the National Portrait Gallery might well be imposed henceforth in the Abbey.   We all know what Rogers, with his cool common sense, thought of burial in Westminster Abbey.   Speaking of the funeral of Campbell, he 'praised Pope for refusing to be buried there. He thought the sentiment of seeing the poet's tomb in the village churchyard so much more valuable than seeing it among a crowd of vain candidates for fame in the Poets'

Corner.' He himself is buried at Hornsey, Lamb not far off at
Edmonton, Hood at Kensal Green, Keats in Rome. But the
list of such anomalies would be interminable. Why should
Burns be here and not Byron? why Sheridan and not Shelley?
why Grote and not Green? It is but too easy to ask un-
answerable questions. If any good could come from directing
attention to the subject it would have come long ago, for if
there is one thing of the kind on which the press is practically
unanimous it is this.

We must not end with fault-finding. The anxiety of the
Dean and Chapter to do what is right must be fully acknowledged, at the same time that we deplore the limited means at
their disposal. There is no shrine in Europe so sacred to the
patriots of the country as Westminster Abbey to ourselves.
The Pantheons and Walhallas of which we so often hear are
but imitations. The continuity of our history is exemplified
in the most tangible manner by this one church, and, in spite
of mistakes and misfortunes, it continues to be, more than
any one other spot, the centre of England and of the British
Empire.

THE END.

Richard Clay & Sons, Limited, London & Bungay.

Price £1 1s. 0d. Cloth. Super Royal 4to. Large Paper Copies, £4 4s. 0d.
Also a Cheap Edition, Large Crown 8vo, cloth, 7s. 6d.

WESTMINSTER ABBEY

BY

The Rev. W. J. Loftie

*AUTHOR OF "A HISTORY OF LONDON," "THE INNS OF COURT
AND CHANCERY," "WINDSOR CASTLE," &c. &c.*

The book contains Twelve Large Copper-plates
and many other Illustrations from original drawings
by HERBERT RAILTON and REGINALD BLOMFIELD,
and from photographs taken specially for this work.

Subjoined is a list of the large Plates :—

WESTMINSTER ABBEY FROM DEAN'S YARD. . *By H. Railton*
SOUTH TRANSEPT OF WESTMINSTER ABBEY . *By H. Railton*
THE CONFESSOR'S CHAPEL . . . . *By H. Railton*
HENRY VII.'S SHRINE . . . . *After Hollar*
WESTMINSTER ABBEY FROM THE NORTH-EAST *By H. Railton*
NORTH AISLE OF THE CHOIR . . . . . . *By H. Railton*
THE NORTH TRANSEPT . . . . *By H. Railton*
THE CHAPTER HOUSE . . . . *By H. Railton*
HENRY VII.'S CHAPEL (EXTERIOR) . . . . *By H. Railton*
SOUTH AISLE OF THE CHOIR . . . . . . *By H. Railton*
HENRY VII.'S CHAPEL (INTERIOR) . . . . *By H. Railton*
THE INTERIOR OF THE NAVE . . . . . . *By H. Railton*

BY THE REV. W. J. LOFTIE

Super Royal 4to.   Price 21s. cloth.
Large Paper Copies (100 only), 42s.

THE INNS OF COURT AND CHANCERY

With Twelve Copper-plates and many other Illustrations
chiefly by HERBERT RAILTON.

"Few writers are better qualified than Mr. Loftie to do justice to these
several sources of interest, and the execution of his congenial task is
admirably furthered by Herbert Railton."—*Times.*

Price 6s. cloth.

WINDSOR CASTLE

With a Description of the Park, Town,
and Neighbourhood.

Third Edition.

With many Illustrations chiefly by HERBERT RAILTON.

"Remarkably pleasant and comprehensive, ... the illustrations are
as finished as the text."—*Guardian.*